I0172832

Success Is Yours

To Keep

The World's best Formula for Success

By Paul Keta

Motivational Books for Entrepreneurs

First published in South Africa in 2015

Copyright 2015- Paul Keta

ISBN   978-0-620-65032-8(e-book version)

        978-0-620-65031-1   (print version)

This book is sold subject to the conditions that it shall not, by way of trade or otherwise, be lent, resold, hired out or otherwise circulated without the publisher's prior written consent, in any form of binding or cover other than that in which it is published and without a similar condition including this condition being imposed on the subsequent purchase

Edited by: Jane Chirchir - Osoro

Eldoret, Kenya

[2]

This book is dedicated to the Lord and my Saviour Jesus Christ who provided the Grace to get this project initiated and to my two lovely daughters Paula Keta and Chelsea Keta who contributed their ideas to writing of this book.

Table of Contents

Chapter 1

About this book

"The one inside of you is greater than the one on the outside"

Life

1   About this Book

1.1   Purpose of this Book

As human beings we grow up with a natural desire to be successful in life thereby driving us to go to school, get an academic certificate, get a professional qualification and hopefully climb up the corporate ladder in the work place. This has been the trend that is assumed to bring in money, wealth, confidence in life and perhaps success in general. When we look at the world at large we notice that there is quite a good number of people who have followed this trend successfully, and made it to the top especially in developed countries. However there is still a large number of our black brothers and sisters in Africa, still trailing behind this chain of success. A few of these blacks end up employed at middle management levels in most companies or even remain unemployed. It may therefore be concluded that black Africans still have to master the art of creating success in life especially given the levels of indigence in the continent.

The purpose of this book is to bring awareness to the black citizens of Africa about the crucial link between success and the unique life purpose of a person.

There has been much talk, much motivational encouragement and much preaching around the importance of people having to know their purpose in life. But there has not been detail or instruction on how people can practically discover their life purpose or achieve the success they want by discovering their life purpose.

This book has been written to assist the black people in Africa with a practical approach to discover their distinctive purpose in life, which in turn is a lever to making their lives successful. Unlike motivational talk-shows where people are advised to find their purpose in life, this book actually provides details on methods, tools, techniques and processes that people can use in order to find out what their purpose in life is. The book provides a formula to both the identification and fulfilment of life purpose which are the key ingredients to successful lives.

This book will stimulate one's mind, exhorts and helps to dispel fear from people who have a will to achieve success in life but continue to experience bottlenecks, roadblocks, and various other limiting challenges in life.

The book provides a roadmap about the journey of life and it aims to:

- Create order in lives of people
- Bring clarity of purpose in lives of people
- Encourage people to do what they were created to do
- Inspire people to become what they were created to be
- Unleash the power inside of people by understanding that we have all the power that we need inside of us to create the lives that

we dream of "The one who is in you is greater than the one who is in the world", 1 John 4 verse 4

- Give hope to people who are facing trials and challenging moments in life
- Bring success to mankind, predominantly my black Brothers and Sisters in Africa

Discovery of life purpose forms the central theme of this book based on the premise that, life purpose is the lever to success in life. The book goes to demonstrate how you can use a combination of tools and techniques to discover or identify your life purpose. The book also clarifies how you can fulfil your own life purpose by following the process of combining a vision, mission and life strategy for your own life leading to an orderly, successful and fulfilling lifestyle. The book further shows you how to formulate a plan for your life in a similar way to a plan for a business, remembering that life of a business has a similar life-cycle to that of a human being as both go through stages of concept, birth, growth, stability, decline and eventually death.

[13]

This book guides you in walking the journey of discovering your unique life purpose which will then enable you to achieve tremendous success based on the simple logic that there is no way a human being, or any other being for that matter, can fail when operating in their area of purpose. This book is about what makes people become great and successful. The book is about human uniqueness, self-discovery, self-actualization and the book acts as a source of inspiration to those who want to get to their unique destiny in life by discovering and fulfilling their unique purpose on Earth.

This book simplifies the process of purpose discovery as it makes reference to practical guidance in the use of tools, techniques, processes and motivational quotes that people can use to assist them to discover their unique purpose in life. The book also contains examples of exceptional people who went further to demonstrate their human uniqueness by fulfilling the purpose of their lives.

Unless otherwise stated, all scripture quotes in this book are taken from either the New International Version (NIV) Bible or King James Version (KJV) Bible.

1.2 Targeted Audience

This book targets mostly emerging Entrepreneurs in Africa. These fall into the lost, the perishing and disillusioned, also referred to as LPD.

LPD largely comprises of people with typically the following kinds of self-limiting characteristics:

- Those gripped with fear and are afraid to make the next move in life e.g. fear to start a business which in turn could be a platform for success
- People who pity themselves, who have no confidence and who prioritize on self-doubt
- People who are not satisfied with their achievements despite putting in reams of effort into their business or personal undertakings
- Those who feel trapped in employment and have no idea how to break out into a free life
- Those who struggle to come up with concepts or ideas to grow their businesses

- Those who are generally tired and have become hopeless about life but cannot figure out how to think out of the box to reach the next level

- People who have not yet fully developed spiritual awareness

- Deep soul searchers

- Those who need to know the reason for their being

- People experiencing chaos in life

- Those who need motivation to succeed in life

- Entrepreneurs who seek success and breakthrough in their businesses

- Those who generally want to set themselves free from bondages in life

The list is endless and is all based on lack of clarity of purpose. The above groups of people will strongly benefit from this book.

[17]

Christians will find it easier to apply lessons learnt in this book given that most of the content points to spiritual and religious experience.

Enjoy your reading

Chapter 2

Introduction

"Let us make man in our own image, after our own likeness"

Life

2 Introduction

2.1 Preface by Paul Keta

Life Coaching fascinates me because it involves dealing with human lives, human souls and human minds, which is the highest level of creation in this world. When I was a child I never dreamt of becoming a Life Coach but due to challenges in life I found myself in a situation where I spent more than eight years researching, studying and trying to understand the purpose of my life.

"What is the purpose of my life?" is a question I would hear people in general and some churches talk about, but it did not mean much to me at all. The more I researched into this subject, the more I felt a deeper hole or emptiness inside of me. I came up with more questions than answers, questions like; Who am I really? What is the meaning of life? What is my meaning in life? Why am I struggling to achieve my goals? Why does it seem like some people have it easier to create success in their lives than others? Are some people created with better gifts than me? Is this because of my African race or is my race cursed? I could hardly find any satisfactory answers to all of these questions.

Over my professional career life that spans more than twenty five years to this date of writing this book, I developed skills in computer systems and electrical engineering. Despite using these skills to make a living I still felt incomplete in many ways. The money I was getting out of using my computer and engineering skills proved to be inadequate on many occasions. Yes the money could provide basic necessities such as food and entertainment, but it never even came close to helping in addressing any of the life questions above.

A time also came in my life when I envied a lot of other people. These are people who sounded very wise when discussing in groups, people who displayed lots of charisma based on their confidence and success in life, people who seemed to naturally take leading roles in work places, in business and so on. I thought that by imitating these people I would also be able to build on my own fascinating and successful character and be able to perform and be as attractive in groups as them, but my, was I wrong... nothing worked. The outcome was acute ups and downs in life, in business and even in relationships, causing severe rising and falling in my life.

This is what then prompted me to embark on a journey, a journey of deep soul searching, a journey of self-discovery, a journey of self-mastery, a journey of self- actualisation, a journey that eliminates a masked character, a journey that confirms what it means to me when the Lord says in Genesis 1 verse 26, "Let us make man in our own image, after our likeness" [2], a journey that eliminates fear in life, a journey of seeking and confirming my purpose and a journey that guarantees success in life.

As I walked this journey, conducting all sorts of research about my life and careful not to make many assumptions and rushed conclusions about the purpose of my life, a pattern gradually emerged, and this was a pattern of a number of characteristic attributes that all pointed out to one thing, one purpose. I discovered and confirmed seven key characteristic attributes about my life that are also applicable to every other human life

Attribute	Description
Natural gift	That I possess a natural gift that has been given to me by Creation. A natural gift is an aptitude which every human being has that comes naturally by birth. I have been carrying and using this gift over all the years of my life but without knowing anything about it. Every human being has one such natural gift and this book helps you to figure out yours. [3]
Personality	That I have a unique personality. This is a distinctive character or

qualities of a person that usually separates them from the rest. Every human being has such a unique personality and this book helps you to figure out yours

Habit	That I have a natural habit. This is a regular tendency or practice that is purely based on my unique personality. Every human being has such a habit from childhood and this book helps you to figure out yours
Passion	That I always experience a burning uncontrollable emotion inside of me each time I get involved in activities that are in line with the desires of my heart. Every human being naturally has an area they are passionate about and this book helps to demonstrate how to figure out yours.

Purpose	That I have an intention to act on life based on a combination of the above character attributes which add up to my purpose in life. Every human being has one such unique purpose in life and this is the most important attribute. This book helps you to figure out your own life purpose.
Mission	That I have a personal assignment in life. The assignment indicates the activities that I have to carry out regularly to benefit other people in the world as I work towards my purpose. Every human being has one such assignment (also called mission) and this book helps you to figure out yours.
Vision	That I carry a unique picture in my mind about my future state of achievements in the long term stretching maybe into ten years

and beyond. This is the vision of my life and every human being can develop one such vision of life and this book helps you to define yours

---

For me to realise and conclude on the discovery of my life purpose I had to take the process a step at a time by starting to look at my natural gift.

Step 1 – My natural gift

Through tools and techniques explained in Section 7 of this book I learnt that the natural gift given to me by Creator is that of "administration" or "management". In other words the purpose that I have in this life and all the things that I effectively do for other humans are based on this gift of administration/management. This is the free gift that God gave to me when I was born. In later sections of this book you will notice how this gift is consistently applied to all the things that I do in this life as I carry out the purpose of my life. I would say that knowing the natural gift given by God is the key success factor in determining one's life purpose. Please refer to Section 7.2 for more detail on how to discover your own natural gift and how the gift applies to all the activities you carry out in helping mankind.

Step 2 – My unique Personality

There are innumerable things that different managers/ administrators do and there are millions of people who have this natural gift of administration/management however there is always distinguishing factors for each of us who have this gift. In my case my distinguishing factor is that I am very good with planning. I want my activities well planned ahead of time. I cannot effectively function without a plan. Plans bring sanity into my life. I have been doing this all the time in my career as a management consultant. I confirmed this on numerous occasions by using a technique called DISC profiling [4]. DISC profiling is (Dominance, Influence, Steadiness and Compliance), as detailed in sub-Section 7.3 of this book and it confirmed to me that I am a planner, a theorist and a designer of things yet to come. This is what separates me from other people who also have a natural gift of management or administration.

Step 3 – My natural habit

It also came to my realisation that all the while in my life I have had this natural tendency or habit of putting things in order, be it in managing project teams in my workplace, the setup in the office, arrangements in my car, organisation of my clothes in the bedroom, structure of my work on the computer, the way I dress, and almost in all things around me. It seems I cannot tolerate chaos. Chaos automatically triggers me into taking action to create order. This has been the case since my childhood even though I was not conscious of it. I can safely conclude that I have a natural habit of creating order.

There is no one way scientific formula to analyse one's habits. This part is based on self-observation. Information can also come based on comments from other people who can tell what your habit is.

I then safely came to a conclusion that, broadly stated, my life purpose is centred on creating order.

After analysing and confirming the above three attributes I came up with a formula that can assist in broadly stating what life purpose is. To get a broad understanding of my own life purpose at this stage I analysed the common thread on the three items described above, thus giving a formula which is:

{Natural habit + DISC profile + natural gift} = broad life purpose statement. This formula can be applied by anyone.

For me, the common thread here is "creating order". Creating order is my habit. Creating order is part of my "planning attribute" of my DISC profile. Creating order is part of my managerial/administrative gift.

This is how I arrived at a conclusion that the purpose of my life is broadly centred on "creating order". Since life purpose always has to do with serving other people then it means that my life purpose is broadly centred around "creating order in lives of people" Writing this book for example is based on my quest to create order where there is chaos in the life of the reader of this book.

Please note that I keep using the term "broadly" above because the purpose statement still needs to be narrowed down further for more effectiveness.

Step 4 – My Passion

To take it a step further I considered the fact that the world has more than seven billion people and it is not feasible for my purpose to be of use to this entire population. So I segmented my target population into a group of people who are specifically linked to my area of passion. This group of people comprises of entrepreneurs. I define entrepreneurs as people who have a will to start doing business, those who are already in business and those that generally want to experience self-actualisation in their lives. Almost everyone has the potential to be an entrepreneur, with creative abilities, only that the majority of people would not have reached that level of self-actualisation to realise their entrepreneurship potential. My strong and burning passion is towards entrepreneurship. This has been the case since I was in primary school where I would build toys and sell them. This passion has never left me since and has seen me starting multiple business ventures, in different parts of the African continent. In social circles my discussions are mostly business related topics. I used an online questionnaire to confirm my passion of entrepreneurship. The approach is more detailed in sub-Section 7.4 of this book.

I also went a step further to segment these entrepreneurs into a smaller group; that is entrepreneurs in Africa, particularly black entrepreneurs in Africa. This becomes the group that my passion is directed towards.

So I was able to narrow down my purpose statement to specifically cater for this targeted group of people even though the purpose statement is still applicable to mankind in general.

Step 5 – My Life Purpose Statement

Combining steps 1, 2, 3 and 4 enabled me to conclude on my life purpose statement as that of:

"Creating order and growth in the lives of entrepreneurs".

This is what I am born to do and will be doing for the rest of my life.

Step 6 – My Life Mission

By definition a life mission is an assignment, a mandate or a task that one has to carry out while here on Earth. It is a statement that describes the daily activities that you carry out in order to meet your purpose. In my case I derived my mission by answering the following questions:

-   What do I do daily in order to achieve my purpose of creating order in lives of entrepreneurs?
-   What methods do I use in carrying out this assignment or how do I carry out the assignment?

By answering the above I crafted my mission statement to be:

"to help entrepreneurs clarify their life purpose and use it to develop strategies for success of their businesses"

If I were to do it daily then I would be:

- **Helping entrepreneurs clarify their life purpose** through coaching sessions, motivational sessions and distributing coaching content on media {*note that the gift of management/administration is at work*}

- **Helping entrepreneurs clarify their life purpose** by ensuring that their life purpose is aligned with strategies that lead to success of the entrepreneurs' business. {*note that the gift of management/administration is at work*}

Step 7 – My Life Vision

Vision is the long term result of continuing to carry out daily work defined in the mission statement. Vision is a mental picture that represents or defines the end-state of achievement assuming all the planned work has been completed and all planned outcomes accomplished.

My aim is to create a centre of small business excellence that continuously rolls out successful entrepreneurs in Africa. In my mental picture I see thousands of successful and prosperous entrepreneurs in the next five years, hundreds of thousands in the next ten years and millions in the next fifteen years. The reality of this is not there yet, but that is what my mental picture sees in the long run as I continue to create orderly and purposeful lives. An orderly life simply points to having clarity as to what one's life purpose is and living life based on that purpose. There has to be order in all things for them to work effectively. This even applies to lives that are seemingly chaotic e.g. Storm Chasers, Doctors etc. there is order in that chaos and it is through order that success can be guaranteed; anything else can be called miracles. We are created in the image of a God of order, a God who knows no chaos and who gave us the ability to operate in His likeness.

2.2 Background

It has been mentioned in various circles of society that the greatest tragedy of life is not dying but rather living a life without purpose, while the most invigorating thing in life is to know the reason why the Lord created you and sent you here on Earth.

This became a headline of discussion among my colleagues in the office. The discussion involved questions like: why is it that some people always seem to enjoy their lives while others seem not to? This was coupled with comments like, "If you do not know who you are then how do you expect to know what it is that you are expected to do," and "if you do not know where you are going then how do you expect to get there?" and "why is it that some people become more prosperous much easier and quicker than others?"

In the journey of my life, it also came to my realization that money, sex, relationships, a good job, substances, playing sport etc. may provide momentary satisfaction, but they are not key ingredients to achieving full happiness and success.

So what does it take to enjoy life with fullest success? It is simple. The answer lies in self-discovery, self-actualization and realization of the purpose for which one is here on Earth. While the answer is simple, the challenge however is in the process involved in identifying one's life purpose and formulating a plan for a successful life based on that specific purpose. Discovery of one's life purpose is one of the most elusive undertakings humans face in life today.

It is because of these mysteries and challenges that I decided to write this book as a debut to a series of books on the subject of Life Purpose

Chapter 3

Terminology

"The blessing of the Lord makes one rich, and He adds no sorrow with it"

Life

3   Definition of Key Terms

3.1   Definition of a Successful Life

People see, experience and define successful life in many different ways. A successful life to one may not be a successful life to another person.

I have tried to define a successful life from my point of view as follows and making reference to Scripture where applicable:

A successful life means living a blessed life where the blessing(s) enables one to achieve one's purpose in life.

A successful life is evidenced by the following signs among others:

- Abundance in financial wealth and prosperity. Total financial independence. Not borrowing but lending, not chasing after money but money chasing after you

- Abundance in material possessions

- Good health

- Good and beneficial social relationships

- Good and loving marriage and family relationships

- Spiritual growth and wisdom

- Love towards others, as Scriptures encourage

- Ability to give to others, as Scriptures encourage

- Fruitfulness and ability to multiply in business and in personal life

- Basically a life lacking nothing and full of joy and happiness. "The blessing of the LORD makes one rich, and He adds no sorrow with it". Proverbs 10 verse 22. [1]

- A legacy based on a purpose and long term vision and this legacy can span into several generations of family descendants to come

3.2   Definition of Life Purpose

In order to define life purpose more meaningfully and in a simplified way, reference can be made to figure 1 below which depicts two scenarios about purpose, i.e. scenario 1 and scenario 2

Fig 1- A purpose illustration

Scenario 1 – This scenario represents a situation where a work supervisor requests a tradesman to carry out a certain task that involves driving twenty nails into a door frame of a building. Due to shortage of resources the supervisor tries to improvise by giving this tradesman a few pebbles to use to drive the nails. As the supervisor leaves to attend to other work he gives the tradesman approximately thirty minutes to carry out this work. He expects the work to have been completed by the time he returns to check on progress. The supervisors then gets back in thirty minutes as agreed with the tradesman and guess what the supervisor is likely to find, a frustrated, unmotivated and stressed tradesman due to failure to complete the assignment, and why is it so?

Scenario 2 – This scenario represents a similar work situation where the supervisor gives another tradesman the same task of driving twenty nails into a door frame of a building and the work is to be completed in thirty minutes as well. To the second tradesman the supervisor provides a hammer to carry out the job of driving nails, and guess what the supervisor is likely to find when he returns after thirty minutes? He will find a joyful tradesman who has completed his assignment. The tradesman is satisfied and fulfilled and why is it so?

In scenario 1 the tradesman has failed to drive all the nails simply because he is using pebbles whose purpose is not to drive nails. No matter how hard he tries to put effort using these pebbles his progress in driving nails will be very little. The tradesman may apply as much effort as he desires but he will certainly not get the job done successfully using stones.

In scenario 2 the tradesman is using a hammer whose purpose is to drive nails. The scenario 2 tradesman is successful because he is using a hammer that is created for the purpose of driving nails.

Here we can clearly see that purpose is the reason why something has been created and if that

[45]

"something" is used for the reason why it was created it naturally becomes successful. In other words purpose is the reason why something exists or a reason for being. With us human beings each of us has a purpose in life and this purpose is the reason why the Creator placed us here on Earth. The purpose of one individual is no way similar or same as any other individual regardless of our geographical location on Earth.

Millions of people in this world are living their lives like stones driving nails. They are not aligned with their purpose and are busy doing things that they were not created to do and hence there is stress everywhere, pain, depression, disillusionment, frustration and failure among humans in the world.

Which scenario does your life fall into?

Chapter 4

Self Analysis

"Where there is no vision, the people perish"

♀
Life

4 Analyse Yourself

4.1 A State of Confusion

Many people in today's society find themselves at a point in their lives where they feel burnt out, bored or discouraged with an aspect or aspects of their lives. Entrepreneurs are not an exception. They are aware that they desperately need to change something, have some ideas but find themselves unsure of what to do and how to implement the changes for improvement. They therefore find themselves carrying on in their current situation, more often than not becoming increasingly frustrated with themselves and disillusioned with their life situation. It is like chasing the wind or a dog chasing its tail, where life never becomes fulfilled. I have defined this category of people as the LPD, meaning the Lost, the Perishing and the Disillusioned.

The LPD category comprises of millions of people in this world and let me try to clarify what I mean by the term LPD.

LPD Category	Description
The Lost	These are people who are completely doing the wrong things in their lives. They have no knowledge of who they are or where they want to get to in life. At every point life is a trial and error game resulting in failure after failure and crisis after crisis. Their life is like someone going up against a brick wall Such people are characterized by, lack of knowledge and lack of religious wisdom. Such people easily go astray because they do not have guiding principles or anything to guide them in life Proverbs 21:16 mentions that "A man who strays from the path of understanding comes to rest in the

company of the dead"

The Perishing   These are people who have given up in life for they cannot see where they are going. They are heavily frustrated and have tried all they can in life but nothing seems to work for them.

In such a group of people you find drunkards and drug addicts, prostitutes, criminals etc. They resort to substances in order to occupy or control their minds. The spirits of these people have practically dwindled and their bones dried up. This usually manifests in the physical in terms of poor health, sickness and general bodily weakness, aggression, self-pity etc. People in this group see life as a hopeless exercise.

Proverbs 17:22 describes this human state clearly by saying that "A cheerful heart is good medicine, but a crushed spirit dries up the bones." [1]

The Disillusioned

For these people, life appears to be going in circles. They plan to do something today and in a month's time they are implementing a different plan altogether.

Such people are discouraged most of the time. They feel inadequate to get anything done. If you ask such a person what it is they want to do in life, chances are you will not get any meaningful answer

Proverbs 29:18 describes this state clearly by saying that "Where there is no vision, the people perish" [2]

LPD brings to mind the saying "DEAD MEN WALKING."

Life, from a headsman's cow's point of view I am sure, consists of spending the day grazing, and then going to sleep and dreaming about more grazing the following day. That is normal life for a cow, but not for a human being. A human being is created to dream, to be spurred on by the dream inside him. Humans are the only creatures that can carry a vision, but sadly most people live just like the cow – no vision, no dream, as long as they can place a plate of food on their table. Such is the epitome of misery, for it is better to be dead, than to not have a reason to live. A man without a vision is a walking grave – he has no reason why death should avoid him, and has no reason to avoid death either. Vision can keep you alive. It will spur you on, even against odds that are otherwise insurmountable

There are more people that have perished from lack of vision than from any plague known to mankind, making graveyards the richest places on this planet.

[52]

For without vision man abandons himself to self-destructive tendencies that having a vision would have prevented him from engaging in. It is the power of vision that anchors a man to the future and keeps him from self-destruction.

Without vision, man operates like a ship without a rudder and anything goes. With vision, only those things that are compatible with the vision are acceptable. You can tell a man without vision by the way he lives his life, for there's no man with a vision to be alive until their 80th birthday who can wallow in drunkenness, drug abuse and reckless abandon, in the name of pleasure. The vision itself will be the enemy of such things, or they are the enemy of the vision. The life of a man tells his vision, or lack thereof.

A young man willing to win a beautiful young lady's heart will dress smart, get his life in order, and stop all forms of misdemeanour, until such a time as he wins her. He may have been failing to do all these things all his life, but now he has a vision, a reason to not do them. So then, we may say that the reason people fail to not do certain things in their life is that they do not have reason (vision) enough not to do them. Or, the reason people stop living (perish) is because they do not have a reason (vision) to live.

Do you have a vision that can keep you alive, or are you a dead man walking, perishing by the day?

In order to get out of a state of confusion in life, my encouragement is for people to stop going in circles with their lives and to stop chasing the wind and start living the fulfilled lives that they were created to live. A fulfilled life means you are living according to your purpose in life, you are doing the things that you were created to do in this life. The biggest question is how to find this elusive purpose which will enable you to create a vision, or a dream, which in turn will help you live a meaningful life thus making yourself great?

4.2 Clarification Required

If your life fits in with the above description of "DEAD MEN WALKING," it means your life calls for immediate adjustments. For such a life the recommended approach is for one to realize that one is in an LPD state. This is an acknowledgement that being in the LPD is some kind of bondage that is holding one's life back. The ideal way to get out of this bondage, is for one to deliver oneself or be delivered from this kind of bondage by pursuing to learn, to know and to understand oneself to the fullest, that is to have an understanding of who one is and what one's destiny is. "My people are destroyed for lack of knowledge". Hosea 4 verse 16 [2]

The primary cause of LPD is lack of vision in one's life, and that is basically caused by not knowing one's purpose in life, or should I say, the secret behind revelation of a vision is in knowing the purpose of one's life. This lack of vision has created untold confusion and directionless in mankind. Therefore it cannot be overemphasized that the most important thing is to know your purpose in life, which is the reason for you being on Earth. *"Where there is no vision, the people perish"*. *Proverbs 29 verse 18* [2]

Same thing applies to life of a business where the starting and most important point is to know or define the purpose of the business. The purpose of this business should be a reflection of the purpose of the business owner; it is one and the same purpose. Everything else revolves around that "purpose".

To ease off the burden of discovering your life purpose, it is advisable to firstly accept that you have a purpose in life. Perhaps you're a person whose philosophy does not believe that there is any purpose or meaning to life. This doesn't matter. Not believing that you have a purpose won't prevent you from discovering it; neither will it change the fact that there is purpose in everything. All that a lack of belief will do is make it impossible to discover one's life purpose or simply take longer to do so

Scripture mentions that, "My people are destroyed for lack of knowledge" Hosea 4 verse 16 [2]. If we explore the word "knowledge" we will find that it touches on a wide spectrum of things; however in the context of this book some of the important things to know are the following:

- God's wisdom and the instructions He passed on to people through the Scriptures
- Self-awareness or knowing oneself beyond doubt. This should cover your personality, character, value___preferences, general behaviour in groups or general behaviour especially under pressure
- Your personal assignment on Earth. This is what enables your purpose to be achieved. It is also called a mission
- Your gift in the Spirit, which is basically your natural gift by Creation

Chapter 5

The Difference

"For I know the plans I have for you"

Life

5 What Life Purpose "IS" And "IS NOT"

5.1 What Life Purpose "IS"

What is the purpose of my life is a question asked by many people as they ponder the reasons for their existence. Life purpose is the expression of the reason for being. The reason represents the intelligence which is within all things. For example, it is the power within a seed, when planted in the garden that it grows step by step to the fulfilment of its reason for being. Everything has a purpose, a time and a season. Autumn is a wonderful example of the fulfilment of many plants, as we enjoy the abundance of fruits and vegetables harvested at this time in the cycles of seasons.

The real you is your inner purpose. When you took your first breath of life, you became a living being. The time of birth determines the quality of the power within you and reveals your purpose in life.

[60]

Life is a journey of existence and every journey has a purpose. Put simply, LIFE PURPOSE is the reason why you are here on Earth, the reason why you were born. Each human being has a unique purpose for being here on Earth, in as much as each person has a unique fingerprint, or a unique iris, or a unique vocal code. If you look at it further, you will realise that everything in this world has a purpose, and so do you.

Personally I remember asking myself hard questions like; if I am to die today and then meet up with the Lord in heaven, how will I respond to typical questions like:

- In the period that I placed you on Earth what have you done that benefited my people on Earth?

- Now that you are here in Heaven, what good things does your family and friends remember you for?

Life purpose hinges around how an individual can help mankind become a better people. It is about how you can make the world a better place by serving other people, whether one-on-one, in groups, as nations or behind the scenes. It is about bringing transformation and this transformation is never about promoting yourself, or achieving great fame or fortune, or experiencing more pleasure or amassing great power. It is always about using the resources God gave you. These resources can be the skills you have acquired, the relationships you have built, the experiences you gained, the money you made, the time you spend, the knowledge and wisdom you have gained etc. All these resources are to enable you to make a positive impact in other people's lives.

God's objective is for you to live an outward-looking life. This is the life where you are not worried about yourself but focused on the needs of others and how you can respond to those needs. When you embrace this kind of mind-set then you are set to become influential and successful and God will be on your side to bless you. As soon as you start thinking about the needs and burdens of others and what you can do to alleviate these burdens then you become a blessing to other people. That way you begin to establish your real identity which is your real self; which is a revelation of your life purpose.

To live a purposeful life does not take a lot of formal courses or lots of special skills. All it takes is a heart which is determined and a Spirit that is willing to deal with issues of people around you and in the world.

If finding your life purpose seems like an elusive undertaking, don't panic because in most cases it is. You are not alone. In this book you will find reassurance and practical support for finding and knowing your life purpose or the purpose of your business.

Once your life purpose becomes clear to you, you will naturally get fired up with unimaginable levels of energy and you will put every effort to live according to your purpose. You will find yourself having more than usual levels of energy which you can divert into driving your purpose. Everything else ceases to matter and your focus will only be on activities and decisions that affect your purpose in life. The levels of energy that you will start having are immense was you start working towards your purpose.

It is about feeling that there is real meaning to your life and a reason for what you do. It is having clear direction and a driving force flowing, even bursting out from you, leaving you in no doubt about your value and how best you contribute to society. When it just flows effortlessly, or even rushes out, that is a clear sign, and then you will just know.

It gives you a foundation for knowing your reason for 'being,' rather than just what you are 'doing', giving the difference between Human 'Being' and Human 'Doing'. You will know and feel that your internal compass is directing you coming from a source of higher consciousness.

It is the difference between your answer to the question – **Who Are You?** – As opposed to – *What do you do* (for a living)?

5.2   What Life Purpose "IS NOT"

There is usually a misunderstanding in terms of interpreting what life purpose IS or IS NOT.

The following are examples of what life purpose IS NOT:

- The current job that you are doing is not necessarily your life purpose. If you look at Jesus Christ, he was a carpenter by profession, having been taught the skill by his Earthly farther, and yet Jesus Christ is little known with reference to carpentry

- Prophet Mohammed was a tradesman and yet he is little known with reference to business. So do not always think that your job is your purpose, however in most instances your job may have a link to your purpose

- Nelson Mandela was a professional lawyer but he is little known with reference to law

You were sent to Earth with a purpose to work towards and a mission to fulfill. If you want to be happy and filled with enthusiasm, you have to discover what your purpose and mission are, and organize your life and activities in line with your purpose and mission.

Most people have the wrong idea about their mission. Here are some common misconceptions and the truth about what a mission on Earth is.

There is no such thing as a life mission and everything is just a coincidence.

There is no such thing as coincidence. We were sent down to Earth with a mission: to increase our ability to love. Everybody's mission is unique because of the different ways we go about this. You too have your individual way to spread more love around you.

[67]

Our mission or goal exists outside of us and is waiting to be discovered.

Your mission is inside you, manifested by your natural talents, desires and passions. Look at what excites you. What kind of activities brings joy and satisfaction? What is it that you spent countless hours on as a child? Your mission already exists, it is for you to discover it.

Our life goal is a particular occupation or profession.

Our life goal is not a well-defined activity. It is much broader than a specific career and contains more than how you are making a living. It is a mistake to confuse how you provide for yourself with what your life mission is. It is possible to implement your mission from within your working environment, but it is much larger than that.

Life is on hold until you have discovered your mission.

No need to sit around and wait. You may still be uncertain about your mission in life, but that does not mean your life hasn't started yet or is not significant. Everything you ran into up to this point in your life does have its importance and has brought you to where you are now: on the road of self-discovery and the fulfillment of your mission. Your life mission is continually being revealed to you. It is not a once-off discovery, and then that's it. The search and implementation continues throughout your life. This is exactly what your life is: the ongoing discovery and implementation of your mission.

You have to change in order to be worthy of discovering your mission.

There is no use in believing there is something wrong with you just because you are still searching. Everybody has a specific mission. Everybody is worthy and has the ability of finding his or her life mission. The desire of your soul to fully participate in the world will attract the right circumstances for you, and allow your mission to present it. Moreover, you are already equipped with the talents needed to fulfill your mission. All that is needed is your awareness. All that is needed is for you to un-cover them that means, take them off the shelf and into the center of your life.

You can fulfill your mission by imitating somebody else.

A person's life destiny is strictly an individual matter and thus cannot be imitated or copied. You can be inspired by the courage and perseverance of another, but you cannot live a copy of that person's life. A mission is like a suit in the big wardrobe of life. There is exactly one suit that fits you like a second skin, tailor-made for you only. If you try on the suit made for another, you are making two mistakes. First, your own suit remains in the closet, unused. Second, you have taken the suit of another and are thus taking the wrong place in the switchboard of life.

It is egotistical and arrogant to occupy yourself with your mission.

One has heard many times to be of service to others, help your neighbor and be ready to reach out to those in need. Partly, that is correct. It is not wise to forget oneself and start helping any random person who crosses your path. It is wiser to remember your mission and find out where, when and who it is you need to help.

This kind of help will be all the more efficient and at the same time gives you much more satisfaction. Fatigue and exhaustion is the only result of only helping others while not taking the time to recharge your own batteries.

Finding your mission in life and living accordingly is neither egotistical nor arrogant. It is your first responsibility. Remember: "Love thy neighbor as thyself." This includes loving the self. Living the implementation of your mission radiates enormous amounts of enthusiasm into your environment. This is a significant contribution to the well-being of all lives that you touch.

You can discover your life mission by intellectual analysis.

It is possible to discover your mission by analysis or intellectual considerations (when these are used as guides) however the processes involved are not really prescriptive. Discovery of your mission is rather a step-by-step process of discovery, driven by the attitude of introspection (looking within the self), by following your passions and by looking for fundamental connections in your life. You will really discover your mission by listening to your intuition and by taking your dreams and visions seriously and implementing them into practice.

You will become famous once you have discovered your mission.

Your mission does not necessarily contain fame and popularity. Many people are implementing their mission with a low profile, in their own personal environment. Your success in fulfilling your mission cannot be measured by external signs such as riches or glamour. The real criteria for measuring successes are enthusiasm, joy, energy, satisfaction, the knowing that everything has its meaning and the feeling that you are in the right place doing the right thing with the right people and overall fulfilling God's mandate in your life.

Pursuing your life goal is hard and difficult.

Sometimes, while pursuing your life goal, you will have moments of fear, doubt and anxiety. You might often wonder if you've made the right choice, and if you couldn't have just kept things the way they were. But as you come closer to fulfilling your life goal, these doubts and fears will be replaced by enthusiasm, joy, happiness, satisfaction and the feeling that life has deeper meaning.

While it is true that some people can find **their life purpose** easier than others, it is also true that God does have a plan for every single person, even if it takes a while to see what the plan is. The Bible mentions in Jeremiah 1 verse 5 [1] – "Before I formed you in the womb I knew you, before you were born I set you apart..." It also mentions in Jeremiah 29 verse11 –

"For I know the plans I have for you, plans to prosper you and not to harm you, plans to give you hope and a future". [1]

Most people think finding your life purpose only means doing something you truly love. It is being in an area that is natural to you where things just fall into place naturally. But what if things are not so clear for you? What if you are not sure what your gifts are? What if you have not discovered any particular hint that makes you think it could be your true calling in life? Or what if you are working somewhere and you are so good at it, but you just don't feel fulfilled? Is this all there is for you?

Don't panic. You're not alone. There are lots of people in the same boat such as the disciples were before Jesus Christ came onto the scene. They were fishermen, tax collectors, farmers, etc. They must have been good at what they were doing because they were feeding their families and making a living.

But then they met Jesus Christ and their true calling immediately came into focus. What the disciples didn't know is that God wanted them to be happy—

even more than they did. And following God's plan for their lives made them happy inside, where it matters. Do you suppose it could be true for you too? That God wants you to be truly happy and fulfilled even more than you already do?

Chapter 6

Discovery

"Love one another"

Life

6 Discovering Your Life Purpose

Discovering and confirming life purpose is the most elusive task to mankind today hence the existence of the LPD population. This book describes the steps that are useful in finding your life purpose. All you have to do is to read it, practice and master the steps.

In the Bible Jesus Christ told His disciples they were supposed to love one another as He loved them "A new command I give you: Love one another. As I have loved you, so you must love one another" John 13:34-35 [1]. This is a very important scripture. Getting good at this part of shaping up life is similar to building the foundation of your house. You wouldn't dream of moving forward without a rock solid foundation. Discovering the purpose for your life is exactly the same. The foundation of the process means getting good at understanding principles of the kingdom of God or generally being a good and effective Christian. Yes, that means being good to

[78]

people even when you don't feel like it, forgiving people, and oh yes, loving the unlovable people in the world. This is simply so because life purpose is about serving other human beings based on love.

It is about how you can *improve on God's creation and make His people better based on love*.

So, what do all the things I have mentioned have to do with what I am supposed to be when I grow up? Everything. When you get good at being a Christian, you also get good at hearing from God. He is able to use you. He is able to work through you. It is through that process that you will get more spiritual guidance that is required in discovering your true purpose in life.

But What about Me and My Life? So if you become great at being a Christian, or at least you think you are, and you still haven't found that true purpose—then what? Getting great at being a Christian means you stop thinking about *you* all the time. It means you take the focus off you and look for ways to be a blessing to others.

There is no better way to receive help and direction in your own life than to focus on someone else. This is completely the opposite of what the world tells you.

After all, if you are not looking out for yourself, then who will? Well—that would be God.

When you focus on someone else's business, God will focus on yours. It means planting seeds in great soil, and then simply waiting for God to bring a harvest into your life while in the meantime do the following...

Step Out and Try It. Working with God to find your life purpose means working as a team with Him. When you take a step, God takes a step

Be willing to try things that interest you. You will know quickly if you have found the right thing for you. Doors will either open or slam shut. Either way, you will know where you stand.

Be Patient. Wanting to know everything *right this second* is common these days. Learning to trust that God will show you when He is ready is a cause for concern to many because this takes patience. God is not going to show you every piece of the puzzle all at once. If he did, you would be overwhelmed by it and get confused at the same time. Not to mention you would be tempted to come up with a back-up plan, "just in case" things did not work.

Do not waste your time on things you know are not from God. "Get rich quick" schemes never work. Finding a Christian husband or wife won't happen if you're focused on activities and events that don't involve Christians. Participating in things you know are wrong—well, you're simply prolonging your answers because revelation of purpose is a big blessing and blessings hardly show themselves in the midst of sins.

Do not let the people around you talk you into many things. Just because it all sounds like a good idea from the world's point of view doesn't mean it is God's plan for you. Following God's leading guidance sometimes means you have to say "NO" to many well-meaning family members or friends. It comes down to the decision to follow, no matter where it leads. Jesus said "Whoever is not with me is against me, and whoever does not gather with me scatters". Matthew 12:30 [1]

Lastly, do not ever give up. You may not know your specific purpose today or tomorrow, but as long as you're great at being a Christian, and your heart is open, you will eventually find God and He will find you because "He is a rewarder of those who diligently seek Him", Hebrews 16:11 [2]

Chapter 7

Techniques

"Plans to prosper you and not to harm you"

Life

7   Techniques to Discover Your Life Purpose

Discovering your Life Purpose is an individual journey.

How do you know? How do you get clear direction? It is an individual path. Some of you will just know and others will need to go through a lengthy process to find your life purpose.

Is it automatic that success comes after discovering purpose? The answer is "No". Creating a successful life is a journey which takes maybe a several months for some and probably years for others. It took me about eight years to understand my purpose in life and several other years to have the confidence to start working towards achieving my purpose. I do not regret those years because I now see them as an investment into my life.

Below are techniques, tools and processes to use in identifying life purpose. Be advised that all the tools and techniques deal with invisible aspects of a human being and this could justify the complexity involved in the subject of life purpose.

7.1   Technique One: God's Direction

I recommend that everyone takes this route first and foremost. The best and most effective way to identify life purpose is to consult the one who created you. I am not referring to parents here because they are just tools for getting the job done, but I am referring to the Lord who planned your presence on Earth before you were born. "Before I formed you in the womb I knew[a] you, before you were born I set you apart"; Jeremiah 1 verse 5. And also as mentioned in the Bible, Jeremiah 29 verse11, God said "For I know the plans I have for you," declares the LORD, "plans to prosper you and not to harm you, plans to give you hope and a future. ..." The question is "do you know these plans yourself?" The key to get answers on this is prayer for God to reveal these plans for you. Because of His sovereignty God can only reveal His purpose in your life when He wills, however there is always guarantee that your prayers will be answered eventually and gradually.

In addition to prayer, there are other various tried and tested techniques and exercises used to assist in discovering the purpose of your life. These techniques and exercises do not give you a prescriptive answer but will guide you into a direction in which you can confirm to yourself what your purpose is. These techniques and exercises are more about self-learning.

7.2   Technique Two: Natural Gift Analysis

The Bible says that God created us in His own image, man and woman. This image of course is a spiritual image. If God exists in the spirit, and He created us in His image it then means we are spirit human beings. The flesh is only there to enable our spirits to carry out physical work while in this world.

If God created us as spirits, it then means that God replicated Himself in humans and each of us carries a special attachment or gift from God in spirit form. These gifts that human beings possess are collectively known as spiritual gifts. Christians are quite familiar with this term of spiritual gifts of God. Spiritual gifts probably contribute the most in defining the life purpose of a human being.

Has it ever occurred to you that in almost all instances when Scripture talks of heroes and successful people of pre-history (from patriarchs to present day heroes) it uses phrases such as, "when the Spirit of God came upon him" or "he was filled up with the spirit of God". This implies that the spirit of God is the one dominantly active in our lives.

Now a few thoughts about how we determine what spiritual gifts we have. There are several approaches to this: 1) written tests, surveys and inventories, 2) self-analysis based on interests and experiences, and 3) confirmation from people who know you well. All three approaches can be helpful, and it is especially helpful if all three lead to the same answer. But none of the three is infallible.

Some of the written inventories are simply a method of analysing yourself and others' opinions about you. The questions might go like this: What do you like to do? What have you done well? What do other people say that you do well? What kinds of needs do you see in the church? (This last question is based on the observation that people are usually most aware of the needs that they are able to help with. For example, a person with the gift of compassion will think that the church needs more compassion.)

Often, we do not know our gifts until we have put them to use and seen whether we do well in that type of activity. Not only do gifts grow through experience, they can also be discovered through experience. That is why it is helpful for members to occasionally try different areas of service. They may learn something about themselves, as well as helping others.

Those are a few comments about gifts in general. But for the rest of this section, I want you to have a look at the questions that are used to enable you to confirm your spiritual gift.

Do not try to answer these questions directly from this book. Instead I developed an online version which is accessible on www.team6.co.za. The questions that are listed in the second paragraph below and are part of the model that I developed to help people identify their purpose in life. The model is called PRASI model and this acronym represents "Purpose Realisation And Self Identity" model. PRASI model will be referred to in all the purpose identification exercises. You can follow these steps to complete the gift questionnaire:

Browse website www.team6.co.za
Highlight "Leadership" from the main menu.
Click "PRASI model" from the menu.
Click "Natural gift" from the diagram.

This online version will provide you with options to select your responses and then the system will automatically work out your natural gift answer which will be shown to you on a website browser. You are free to try this exercise as many times as you want in case you are not satisfied with the answers. The answers will also indicate the areas of service in which you can use this spiritual gift. It also indicates the dangers that go with any of the spiritual gifts.

Here is the list of questions as they will appear online.

1. I enjoy presenting God's truth in an inspired and enthusiastic way.

2. I am always ready to overlook my own personal comfort in order that the needs of others may be met.

3. I find great delight in explaining the truth of a text within its context.

4. I am able to verbally encourage those who waver and are spiritually troubled.

5. I am able to manage my financial affairs efficiently so that I can give generously to the Lord's work.

6. I find it easy to delegate responsibility and organise others towards spiritual achievement.

7. I readily find myself sympathising with the misfortune of others.

8. I am conscious of a persuasiveness of speech when encouraging people to examine their spiritual motives.

9. I have the knack of making people feel at home.

10. I delight in digging out facts concerning the Bible so that I can pass them on to others.

11. I have a deep concern to encourage people toward spiritual growth and achievement.

12 I am cheerful about giving material assets so that the Lord's work can be furthered.

13. I am able to effectively supervise the activities of others

14. I enjoy visiting those in hospital or the shut-ins.

15. I am able to present the Word of God to a congregation of people with clarity and conviction.

16. I am happy when asked to assist others in the Lord's work.

17. I am concerned that truth should be presented in a clear fashion with proper attention to the meaning of words.

18. I am at my best when treating those who are spiritually wounded.

19. I have no problem in joyfully entrusting my asset to others for the work of the ministry.

20. I am able to plan the actions of others with ease and supply them with details which will enable them to work efficiently.

21. I have great concern for those involved in trouble.

22. I find myself preaching for a verdict whenever I present the truths of the Word of God.

23. I delight in providing a gracious haven for guests.

24. I am diligent in my study of the Bible and give careful attention to necessary research.

25. I am able to help those who need counselling over personal problems.

26. I am concerned over the question of financial assistance being available for all sections of the church.

27. I am deeply sensitive to the need of a smooth running administration so that every phase of activity is carried out decently and in order.

28. I work happily with those who are ignored by the majority.

29. I find my preaching brings people to a definite point of decision.

30. I enjoy taking the load from key people so that they can put more effort into their own particular task.

31. I am able to explain well how the Bible hangs together.

32. I am acutely aware of the things that hold people back in their spiritual development and long to help them overcome their problems.

33. I am careful with money and continually pray over its proper distribution in the work of the Lord.

34. I know where I am going and am able to take others with me.

35. I am able to relate to others emotionally and am quick to help when help is needed.

Based on biblical analysis, the following is a list of natural gifts from God:

Natural gifts from God

- Prophesy

- Serving

- Teaching

- Faith

- Giving

- Ruling, Leadership, Administration

- Sympathy/Mercy

I did this exercise on several occasions only to reconfirm that my God given natural spiritual gift is Administration, Rulership, Management or Coordination. As an example, below is the result of a gift of administration.

Description of gift of Administration

Ruling, management or coordination of activities of others for the achievement of a common objective, purpose, goal or vision. An ability to preside or lead, seeing future consequences of one's actions; able to distinguish major objectives and help others visualise them.

The gift of administration is mentioned in I Corinthians 12:28. Administration means to govern, pilot, direct or steer. It was used to describe a person that would steer a ship. A person with the gift of administration is a good strategic thinker, organized, has supervisory skills and manages people and projects well. When directions are set by leadership, this person can help accomplish the job efficiently. The Greek word "kubernesis" means one who steers a ship. This expert had the responsibility to bring a ship into the harbour through the rocks and shoals, under all types of pressures. As an administrator you have the Spirit-given capacity and desire to serve God by organizing, administering, promoting, and leading the various affairs of the church. The administrator is not a glorified file clerk.

As an administrator you are a take-charge person who jumps in and starts giving orders when no one is in charge. You will put a plan on paper and start delegating responsibility. You may lean toward organizing things, events or programs, OR toward organizing people, emphasizing personal relationships and leadership responsibilities. In the first case, you usually organize details and have people carry them out. In the second case, you tend to organize people and rely on others to take care of the little things.

You don't often admit to mistakes and do not like to take time to explain why you are doing things; you just expect the job to get done. If things in the church, office, club, etc. become fragmented, you can harmonize the whole program if given a chance. You are a person with a dream and are not afraid to attempt the impossible. You are goal-oriented, well-disciplined, and work best under heavy pressure. You are often a good motivator and not a procrastinator. You are serious minded, highly motivated, intense, and have an accurate self-image. You tend to be more interested in the welfare of the group than your own desire. You are probably a perfectionist and want things done your way now.

Possible uses of the gift

You may work well as the leader of a project, ministry, or program; chairman of a committee or board; a church planner; or chairman of building or fund-raising projects. Other positions where you may serve well include pastor, assistant pastor,

[96]

business manager, office manager or department head for large staff, Sunday school superintendent, fellowship group or missionary circle leader, library manager, camp director, church moderator, bus ministry director, nursery coordinator or Vacation Bible School director.

Dangers of this gift

- *proud of power over people*

- *using people to accomplish goals*

- *overlooking character faults in those who can be useful to reaching goals*

Although to others you appear to be organized, you usually aren't. Be careful that you do not make decisions just based on logic rather than Scripture. Work on your willingness to admit to making a mistake and on being more sensitive to "little" people. Try to be a little more tolerant of other people's mistakes.

Beware of Satan's attack on your gift. Beware of Satan's attack on your gift. He can cause pride because of your leadership role, selfishness because of success (not sharing glory with those under you), blame-shifting when things go wrong, discouragement and frustration when goals are not met, anger and mistreatment of those who disagree with your plans, lack of concern for people, lack of spiritual growth, and wrong motives

7.3   Technique Three: Your Natural Habit

There is no one scientific formula to analyse one's habits. This part is based on self-observation. Information can also come based on comments from other people who can tell what your habit is. Try to look at natural tendencies from since you were young. The things that you find yourself doing to yourself and to others. We are looking at good habits here and not the likes of habitual smoking, drinking, theft, lies etc.

Typical habits would be smiling, expressiveness, desire to teach, encouragement, convincing, leading, courage, analytical, fitness, etc. There are as many good habits as the population of people in the world

7.4   Technique Four: Your DISC Profile
Be sure about your personality style because personality has a very strong bearing on your life purpose. Personality describes who you are.

This personality assessment is based on the work of Doctor William Marston [5], one of the Psychologists of the twentieth century. Doctor Marston studied the characteristics, patterns and responses of thousands of individuals and as a result developed an assessment to measure four important behavioural factors, commonly referred to on the market as DISC (Dominance, Influence, Steadiness and Compliance) profile. DISC factors can be combined in multiple combinations to give twenty five different personality styles as listed below.

1 Advisor

2 Advocate

3 Assessor

4 Attainer

5 Challenger

6 Chancellor

7 Communicator

8 Concluder

9 Contemplator

10 Designer

11 Director

12 Establisher

13 Governor

14 Influencer

15 Inquirer

16 Leader

17 Logical Thinker

18 Mediator

19 Motivator

20 Peacemaker

21 Persuader

22 Practitioner

23 Precisionist

24 Reformer

25 Technician

You do not have to pick on any of the personality styles listed above just by reading this book. To help understand use of the DISC profiling process, I developed an online assessment that enables you to complete a matrix of statements that will be processed by the website to give you an answer to your personality. The response will also provide greater detail and explanation of your own personality style.

The matrix of the statements is available on website www.team6.co.za.

You can follow these steps to confirm your DISC profile:

- Browse website www.team6.co.za
- Highlight "Leadership" from the main menu.
- Click "PRASI model" from the menu.
- Click "DISC profile" from the diagram.

After completing the matrix of statements the website will provide an answer to confirm your individual personality.

If you carry out the online exercise you will get an automated response that indicates your individual personality. This individual personality must be related to your natural gift as determined in the previous section.

As an example, when I carried out this exercise I was able to confirm my personality profile of "Designer/Administrator or one who creates" based on the feedback below that comes from the website. Check how this tallies with my natural gift of Administration.

Designer/Administrator/One Who Creates

Individuals who are **Designers** exhibit a high task- orientation and are very sensitive to problems. They are creative, determined, and analytical in their approach to effective problem solving, never accepting a "quick fix". Their goals is to have everything correct and in control while simultaneously avoiding failure. Designers are able to initiate change and improvements, because of their administrative skill. Because they sometimes feel that they are only one that can do a job right, Designers will sometimes get bogged down and not allow others to help. Under pressure, they may come across to others as aggressive or stubborn. It is important for Designers to be sensitive to the needs of others around them in order to insure a positive environment. Since Designers value accuracy and precision, high standards are maintained in all aspects of a Designer's work life.

Designers in Scripture:
Bezaleel, Jochebed, Jethro
Scripture Verses to Study
Exodus 35:30-36:8, 37:1-9, Exodus 1:22-2:4, Exodus 2:18

Bezaleel: This man had been handpicked by God to be the chief architects of the temple in Moses' time. Bezaleel's high personal standard would require nothing less than absolute perfection in the construction of God's temple. Exodus 37 verses1-9 recounts the exact steps he took in creating the ark, and he is very precise.

Jochebed: Although Moses' mother is silent in this passage, we clearly see her creative problem-solving skills at work to save her son's life. She knows that her task was to save her son, and stubbornly worked to save him in spite of Pharaoh's order.

7.5   Technique Five: Your Passion

I prepared a questionnaire comprising of fourteen questions as listed at the end of this sub-section. This questionnaire helps you to confirm your area of passion. Do not try to answer these questions directly from this book. To do this exercise you have to use the online version that I developed to enable users to interact with these questions. The online questionnaire is accessible on www.team6.co.za

You can follow these steps to confirm your area of passion:

- Browse website www.team6.co.za
- Highlight "Leadership" from the main menu.
- Click "PRASI model" from the menu.
- Click "Passion" from the diagram.

After completing the online questionnaire, the website will forward an email to you providing you with feedback on your answers. This feedback will be compared with suggested remarks around your purpose. These remarks are already built into the online system. Once you receive this feedback you will be able to analyse some trends and common threads that will point you to your passion. This is an exciting and important part that points you to the desire of your heart. The following are the questions you will see on the website

1   What are you naturally curious about?

2   What would you change about the world?

3   What would you love to do or accomplish before you die?

4   What would you be doing if it was not possible to fail?

5   What would you be doing if you were not limited by money?

6   What would you like to hear about yourself at your funeral?

7   What are the things you currently enjoy doing?

8   What were the activities or tasks you were doing when you felt most empowered?

9   What would you most like to be acknowledged for so far in your life?

10 If you had only one wish, what would it be?

11 Whose life do you want to be living?

12 What ideas are you most inspired by?

13 With whom would you like to surround yourself?

14 Do you take responsibility for what is happening to you?

Chapter 8

Your Purpose

"All these are the work of one and the same Spirit"

Life

8 Your Purpose Statement

Now you have figured out four characteristics about yourself and these are:

- Your natural gift
- Your unique personality
- Your natural habit
- Your passion

To derive a broadly based purpose statement you need to combine the above characteristics as follows:

{Habit + DISC personality + natural gift} = broad purpose statement

In order to narrow down your purpose statement and have it directed towards a particular segment of people you then need to add your passion as follows:

{Habit + DISC personality + natural gift + passion} = LIFE PURPOSE STATEMENT

Having gone through all the suggested techniques in the previous Chapter I can safely conclude that you can now craft up your own unique life purpose statement. To test the effectiveness of your life purpose statement you have to ask yourself questions like; when you help others, how do you do it and do you feel satisfied? What effect does it have on others? Do you help others discover their own truth?

Write Down Your Life Purpose

Set aside time to write down a clearly crafted Life Purpose statement for yourself – one that resonates and has meaning for you. Put it before you in a place(s) where you'll see it often.

The 'Power' of a Clearly Defined Life Purpose

"When you shift into a 'purposeful' state of mind, then all you need in the way of personality characteristics will naturally surface" – Dr. Wayne Dyer. [6]

What this means is that when you're doing what you love and living on purpose, giving of yourself in a joyful way, your personality will reflect that bliss and all it involves.

This will not require struggle or detailed written goals and action plans. You will not require intelligence, skills or confidence from outside of yourself because you'll find these qualities already exist within you.

Your ability to manifest the necessary talent, intellect and mobilize changes in yourself to fulfill your purpose will already be intact.

Knowing Your Purpose Helps You Live With Integrity and In Alignment with Your Life Purpose

[112]

For instance, I know my Life Purpose is creating order in peoples' lives, especially entrepreneurs– to coach and guide people how to improve their lives, from what I learned through my own experiences and what I learnt from gurus of this world

How did I arrive at my purpose? By learning unconditional Self Love first, being selfless, being true to myself, discovering my authenticity, and my unique way to achieving a self-determining life, doing my own thing and finding and following my own passion.

I had to learn these things first before coaching others. If I am to show other people to be truthful with themselves I had to be truthful with myself too.

Learn Self Love first and everything will take care of itself.

When you're inspired by a greater Life Purpose things just start to fall into place for you in your life. Knowing your Life Purpose on the 'big picture' level helps you know how you relate to your life as a whole. Life Purpose serves as a focus around which to direct your life.

"The purpose of life is not just to be happy. It is to be useful, to be honourable, to be compassionate, and to have it make some difference that you have lived and lived well." When life gives you lemons, make lemonade" Ralph Waldo Emerson [7]. It's a wise perspective for life. You have to stop looking at the "lemons" that are coming your way to be problems. Instead, look at them as a wonderful resource that can help you in life.

8.1   Additional Exercises

These additional exercises can be useful if you want to further confirm your purpose statement.

8.1.1   Exercise One: Talents

Talents may easily be confused with gifts of the spirit mentioned in sub-Section 7.2. Listed below are a few highlights summarizing the differences between spiritual gifts and talents:

1   A talent is the result of genetics and training, while a spiritual gift is the result of the power of the Spirit that dwells in us humans, thus giving us special abilities

ii   A talent can be possessed by anyone, Christian or non-Christian, while spiritual gifts are more dominant in Christians especially after they receive or are baptized by the Holy Spirit

iii   Talents come through the genes of natural

[115]

inheritance; gifts directly by the Lord

iv   Talent comes from the first Adam and,
     however attractive, it is still a part of man's
     fallen nature. The gift is given by the Holy
     Spirit, as it pleases Him" 1 Corinthians 12
     verse 11 [1] "All these are the work of one
     and the same Spirit, and he distributes
     them to each one, just as he determines".

While both talents and spiritual gifts should be
used for God's glory and to minister to others,
spiritual gifts are focused on specific spiritual
tasks, while talents can be used entirely for
non-spiritual purposes. There is a big
difference between natural talents and
supernatural gifts.

Below is a more detailed comparison between
talents and gifts.

Talents

- Talents are inherited from one's parents and through genealogy ultimately from the first man, Adam
- Talents are received at birth; they are natural endowments
- Talents are possessed both by saved people and by unsaved people. There are many unsaved people who are very talented (musical ability, artistic ability, athletic ability, mathematical ability, etc.) the term "saved people" is used to refer to born again Christians
- For full effectiveness talents need to be developed. A person who is naturally skilled musically must still learn to play an instrument, often demanding years of practice. Most professional athletes not only have natural talent but they have developed this talent through years of practice and hard work.
- Talents possessed by believers or saved people ought to be surrendered and consecrated to the Lord and used for His

[117]

honour and glory. Example: A skilled organist playing for a worship service "as unto the Lord

- Talents are natural.

Gifts

- Gifts are supernatural

- Gifts are received from God

- Gifts get more pronounced at the time of the new birth or time of getting saved or in those who are members of the church which is called the Body of Christ. An unsaved person might mimic a spiritual gift, but it is counterfeit and limited to self-activity (e.g.-a false prophet, a false teacher, etc.)

- This same man, upon believing on the Lord Jesus Christ, may not receive the gift of teaching. Spiritual gifts are determined by God not by any natural talents which a man may possess. If this same man should receive the gift of teaching it is above and

[118]

beyond and distinct from any natural teaching talent which he had. It is something that he did not have prior to him being born again

- Gifts need to be exercised and this can only happen as the believer stays spiritually healthy and grows "in the grace and knowledge of the Lord Jesus Christ" (2 Peter 3 verse 18). The proper exercise of spiritual gifts requires spiritual growth and maturity (Ephesians 4 verses 13-16)

- Gifts are given by God for the outworking of God's life as expressed by the Body of Christ. When the Body is healthy the life of God is manifested and God is glorified

An important thing to remember is that talent is not your life purpose. However talent plays a role in supporting your life purpose. Given that a talent is based on genes and that genes are unique for an individual it therefore means that genetics play a direct role in defining your purpose which is also unique to yourself. As you work on confirming your talent, think about the suggestions listed below

Think about what you love to do. What do you usually enjoy doing, without being asked? What do you seem to be naturally good at? On what do you focus best or most enthusiastically? What must you be dragged away from doing?

Have fun. Whatever that means to you, let yourself do it. It's not just for children. Experiment, explore, and investigate. Try doing different things and entertain different activities. Even try on taking up different personalities.

Try taking some personality tests. These sorts of tests do not identify talents in and of themselves, but they can lend insights that might provide a solution to part of the puzzle.

Notice what people tell you about yourself. Do they notice that you light up when you explain something? Does everybody seem to compliment you on your writing? Is there something unique about your physical coordination?

Consider your interests. What sorts of things do you like to read about, write about, or talk about?

What shows do you watch on television? What magazine and newspaper articles catch your eye?

Notice what you are not good at, too. What seems always to be a struggle? What makes you feel awkward or out of place? For instance, some people are great talkers but hate writing; for others, it's the other way around. That's not to say you can't develop skills and strategies in areas that are not your forte.

Practice makes perfect. Once you find something you love to do, do more of it. You will improve your skills and refine your technique this way. You will also discover the depths of your talent, whether it was more a passing phase. Even if the interest turns out to be temporary, you may notice what interested you about a particular activity.

Share your talent with others. It is okay to practice by yourself, but at some point, you should nurture your talent by finding a mentor or coach, even if it is just somebody else with more experience at something who can give you advice. Having an audience (even a small one) is, in many cases, equally important.

Use your talent. Make the world a better place.

Below are some examples of people who demonstrated that when talent is utilized to its high level it can make a person very great.

Note that the effects of talent are fairly short-lived. When a person dies the effects of talent can be forgotten within a reasonably short time, unlike the effects of life purpose that keep on multiplying even after the person has died.

- Bill Gates - The greatest "software developer"

- Oprah Winfrey - The greatest "talk-show presenter"

- Mozart - The greatest "musical composer"

- Tiger Woods – The greatest "golfer" of his time

- Pele – The greatest "footballer" of his era

- Bruce Lee – The greatest "martial arts superstar"

- Michael Jackson – The king of pop music

- Bob Marley – The King of reggae music

Examples listed above indicate talents and not life purpose even though these talents in most cases contribute to their life purposes.

8.1.2   Exercise Two: 50 Purpose Statements

Take a piece of plain paper, an A4 size one. Write fifty statements. Each of the statements should start with the phrase "I was born to". Let the thoughts and answers come naturally as you write. As your list grows you will probably start to probe your mind, your spirit and your experiences in life. After completing all the 50 statements then analyse them carefully. You will begin to see a pattern or common thread in your statements. This common thread is a good pointer to your purpose and can help you to confirm the purpose statement you crafted for yourself in earlier Section 8 of this book.

8.1.3   Exercise Three: "I AM" Statements

I assume that you have now built confidence to a point where you have developed or can develop your own life purpose statement. This should now place you in a situation where you describe yourself using the "I am" statements.

Definition of the "I AM" statement

"I AM" represents you. In the burning bush verses of the Old Testament, Moses asked God what he shall say to people when they ask who had sent him. God replied that you should tell them that "I AM" has sent you. Here God is referring to Himself as "I AM" meaning His true being. So if we are Spirits from God, and created in His image and likeness it means that a component of us as humans, which is the spirit, represents the God in us. In almost all situations that we describe and that involve us, we almost always say "I AM" but without paying attention to the use of the word "I AM."

If I meet a colleague and greet him like "how are you today?", the automatic answer that comes from him will automatically start with the words "I AM", for example he will say "I am fine" or "I am not complaining" or "I am good" etc. This "I am" represents the person and who that person is. Then the next question to be asked is "who are you?"

Deep soul seekers revolve around one central question: **"Who am I?"**

Even the business world ponders this crucial matter. According to business gurus, the first step on the road to success is asking this very question: "What's my mission? What on Earth am I doing? Am I in the right place? Who exactly am I?"

If you can't answer these questions, then you are wasting 90% of your precious time and energy doing things that are neither your purpose nor your mission. In such a situation I strongly recommend that you go through the techniques and exercises described in earlier sections of this book.

The question "Who am I?" makes you feel an **inner anxiety**, urging you to search for the deeper meaning of your life.

If you consider life to be painful, if you feel dissatisfied, if you feel "there must be more than this", if you feel out of place in this world, or if you feel that you still belong to LPD then you have neither found purpose of your life nor your identity.

If you are questioning the meaning of life, if you can't find inner peace, if you are not satisfied with choices you've made in life, if you don't know which way to turn, if you feel your life is stuffed with things that aren't of your choosing and that don't satisfy you, if you often feel burdened and bad-tempered, if you "have everything to feel happy" but you still don't, then it is time for you to discover your true self, your true purpose in life.

[127]

Human beings want to feel useful. We long to give our lives some deeper meaning. As long as you have not discovered this **deeper meaning,** you feel frustrated and on the **wrong track and cannot relate to your "I AM" ness.**

We want our lives to be worthwhile. This does not mean we need to achieve 'great feats' or become world famous. We just need to feel in place and do the right thing surrounded by the right people. It's about finding out our mission. It's about finding '**inner peace**' by clearly knowing who we are.

As long as you have not identified your "I AM" ness then you will be wrestling with dissatisfaction, powerlessness, frustrations and fatigue and may other negative influences.

If you are not in touch with your own desires, you will easily fall prey to expectations projected upon you by your environment. If you are not following your own path, then you must be following someone else's! If you are not clear on your own life mission, you will find it hard to say "no" to what other people want you to do. This un-decidedness makes you available for all who cross your path and want a piece of you, draining your energy.

As long as you are not clear on who you are at the core, then you are submitted to others who may not care about what is best for you. Just like disease, these kinds of negative relationships are a manifestation of low-level energy, showing that you have lost focus and have strayed from your own golden brick road. Your self-esteem is probably pretty low and you suffer from serious doubts and fears.

The longer you put off the search, the more the feeling that something is missing will devour you. Your self-esteem will surely decrease.

The best way to rebuild your fragile self and re-establish an inner sense of security is to make the search for your identity and subsequently fully dedicate yourself to it.

Why is this so important? Because you can only find real joy in life by discovering and living according to the unique way of your personal evolution.

But, maybe you think, can't I just continue living life the way I have been all along? My life may not be all that exciting and rosy, but it's still doable. Can't I just try to hang in there and keep the status quo?

The answer is "yes". You can keep living your life in a monotonic, sad, senseless way.

But don't expect any real satisfaction. The need to feel useful is so fundamental that you cannot feel happy as long as you have no clue what you are here for.

[130]

That is exactly the difference between humans and animals. For an animal it may suffice to just sleep, hunt and eat, but humans look for the deeper meaning of life. Humans "know" that we are here on Earth for something more important than just eating, sleeping and working.

I guess this chapter has motivated you enough to go the full way to discovering and defining your "I AM"-ness.

The big hint in crafting the "I AM" statements is to stop thinking of yourself and your capabilities as a human being. In Greek history the term "I am" originated from the name Yahweh, which is one of the names given to God as we know Him in today's English. So imagine that when you say "I AM" you actually replace the term "I AM" with Yahweh.

In other words it is God describing Himself and His capabilities through you. Knowing God as we all do we cannot let His capabilities be limited by our small minds.

I did this exercise for myself and concluded that:

- "*I am the beacon of success*". Whoever comes to me will have direction, clarity and purpose in their life and the life of their business

- "*I am the catalyst for growth*". Whoever comes to me will have motivation and inspiration to transform their life for the better and encouragement to embark on large, lucrative projects without fear.

These statements link quite well with my natural gift, my personality and my life purpose.

For further clarification I could not think of better examples than those given by Jesus

[132]

Christ in the Scriptures as He describes His "I AM"-ness and who He is to mankind. These can guide you into developing your own "I AM" statements

I am the bread of life

"I am the bread of life. Whoever comes to me will never go hungry, and whoever believes in me will never be thirsty". John 6 verse 35 [1]

I am the good shepherd

"I am the good shepherd; the good shepherd lays down His life for the sheep. He who is a hired hand, and not a shepherd, who is not the owner of the sheep, sees the wolf coming, and leaves the sheep and flees, and the wolf snatches them and scatters them"....John 10 verse 11 [1].

I am the way and the truth

"I am the way and the truth and the life. No one comes to the Father except through me". John 14 verse 6 [1]

I am the resurrection and the life

"I am the resurrection and the life. The one who believes in me will live, even though they die". John 11 verse 25 [1]

8.1.4   Exercise Four: TEAMS Profiling

Here is another exercise to help you understand your uniqueness which in turn has a direct bearing on your life purpose. It is called the TEAMS profile [8]

From the largest organization to the smallest workgroup, the value of the team is being recognized and relied upon today more than ever before. The face of business is changing more rapidly than ever before in history. People are reacting to the stress of change and feel a need to come together for strength and security. In some arenas, the use of teams is seen as some sort of ultimate answer to every problem. The slogan "Together Everyone Achieves More" is being hiked from the break room to the board room

An effective team has a natural structure and the team leaders must deliberately place individuals into roles that maximize their personal effectiveness and efficiency. Imagine if you are now placed in a team to play a role that has no link to your purpose. The result will be devastating. It will obviously be like the case of the tradesman using a stone as per our previous illustration.

In this context the term TEAMS is an acronym referring to Theorist, Executor, Analyst, Manager and Strategist. These are the five groups that researchers found to be most effective in any team.

To help you appreciate the effectiveness of TEAMS I have included description of the team role, what value it adds to a team, the core strength of that role and its limitation. You will notice that the TEAMS area that is most applicable is directly linked to your life purpose

I am a Theorist. I enjoy thinking in the abstract. I easily generate ideas to solve problems or to come up with new designs for project concepts.

[135]

This enables me to effectively plan ahead. As mentioned in the introductory section, planning is also my DISC profile.

Theorist

Theorist Role Description

The theorist is the member of the team who generates ideas, models and hypotheses

They have the capability to exhibit high task orientation while remaining very sensitive to problems. Theorists have an innate ability to see problems and situations from different vantage points and thereby develop ideas that may seem to overlook ideas of others. They are creative, determined and analytical in their approach to effective problem solving and are highly unwilling to accept a "quick fix". Theorists initiate changes and improvements. They tend to be determined individuals and are often very sociable. These are the people who excel at thinking outside the box". When they also possess high levels of interpersonal communication skills, they can be very effective at recruiting people to help implement their ideas. Theorists are a source of fresh insights, innovative concepts, inventive and unique approaches and ground breaking proposals. Once the ideas have been generated, Theorists will interact well with Strategists and Analysers to determine the best methods for implementing their ideas.

Key Value of Theorist to a TEAM

Theorists are valued for their ability to move the team in new directions, exploring and defining solutions. They are not afraid of the untried or the unique and tend to move rapidly through a series of several different approaches to move any project or concept forward.

Core Strength of Theorist

Theorists are creative problem solvers. Their primary team strength is their excellent ability to see problems from a new angle. Theorists see solutions that others do not. Their conceptual developments often go beyond the obvious to the unique. They possess an uncanny ability to provide an accurate assessment of the present situation and the necessary steps to follow. They interact very well with Strategists. Theorists are not afraid of new ideas and will often take a thorough and methodical approach to problem solving that examines several possible solutions. Many Theorists have strong, well - developed communication skills. They are able to negotiate conflicts by taking positive action and presenting several options that consider all possible avenues.

Potential Limitation of Theorist

The Theorist loves new ideas, and may have a tendency to focus on generating new ideas rather than focusing on completion. They need deadlines and will benefit from high levels of interaction with other team members who have the ability to help them focus and follow - through.

[138]

When appropriate, their creative energy needs to be directed towards the implementation of their ideas rather than the creation of new ones.

Executor

The Executor is the member of the team who implements the ideas, programs, solutions and initiatives developed by the team. They concern themselves with the process of carrying out and completing the tasks that need to be done. Executors will clarify all expectations and procedures before undertaking new projects, and will appreciate the procedures being in place before they begin to work on them. Once they understand the process, and have taken the opportunity to observe the results and compare them with previous projects, Executors are invaluable sources of information for making beneficial changes to the process. This is because executors often have an extremely clear understanding of the elements that make up the process and are excellent sources of information on bottlenecks, breakdowns, stoppages etc. In sharing processes, process information, Executors may provide some ideas regarding process, but they do not typically see themselves as the source for new ideas for the process. However the Executor will frequently feel uncomfortable volunteering information leading to procedural change, so one of the other team members will need to inquire, preferably in a non-threatening manner. The Executor will be concerned about performing assigned tasks correctly and may take criticism personally. Also, Executors do not characteristically see themselves as "leaders", and prefer not to hold leadership roles

Key value of Executor to TEAM

Executors are valued for their precision, accuracy and accountability. Their motto is "Do things according to plan" They set personal standards for excellence that often exceed others standards but have the ability to carry those standards into the production process. When faced with procedural issues, they are able to solve them logically and methodically. They are naturals at putting the "finishing touches" on the project.

Core Strength of Executor

Their systematic detail- oriented approach to operations is the core strengths of the Executor. This approach often allows them to see impending problems before others might and provide information to better accomplish the task.

Potential Limitations of Executor

The executor tends to adopt a "wait and see" attitude, rather than taking charge of a situation. Seeking their attention at regular intervals is important. Also, Executors need clearly – defined processes and goals in order to be effective.

Analyst

The analysts are the members of the team who extract key elements of an idea and develop the process by which the idea can be implemented. One of the primary values that Analysers bring to the team is their instinctive ability to detect procedural flaws, logical defects, and other potential problems.

Their key strength within the team environment is the ability to examine the plans and programs which the team has developed with an eye towards the additions, deletions or changes that will be necessary to ensure successful implementation. They are unique in that they have a strong combination of people skills and orientation to detail, allowing them to articulate their concepts well in many different areas. They tend to use their communication skills to make sure that each area of a project will get done in the proper order and manner, focusing more on the tasks than the people doing the tasks. Analysers may send ideas back to Theorists, Strategies or Managers several times, fine tuning them and developing an implementation plan that will ultimately work.

Key Value of Analyst to TEAM

The Analyser is valued for precision, accuracy and reliability. Their motto is, "Do things right the first time." Analysers set personal standards for excellence that often exceed others standards. They are thinkers who are able to solve problems logically and methodically with great creativity. Analysers are extremely thorough in all their activities. Their ability to think critically allows them to define a situation systematically and methodically- first gathering then criticizing and testing their conclusions.

Core Strengths of Analyst

Analysers constantly challenge the ideas, procedures and concepts that are currently under consideration. They seek out better means of accomplishing tasks and more efficient methods of performing them. They are orderly and net, and tend to bring that order into chaos of high pressure projects. The team will value their work ethic and the ability to perform well under pressure and tight deadlines.

Potential Limitations of Analyst

The Analyser may tend to get bogged down in the details of the project. When this happens, they may even lose sight of the overall goal. They live in and love the world of ideas, and will sometime challenge and debate simply for the pleasure of the argument. Another potential limitation of the Analyser is their tendency to choose a low risk approach instead of one that may have a higher element of risk with a greater potential return.

Manager

The Manager is the member of the team who facilitates interaction between other team

[144]

members and who oversees the implementation of various aspects of the plan. They tend to be sensitive and have high standards. Decisions are made after the gathering of facts and supportive data. Managers enjoy monitoring processes, interacting with team members, supervising production and otherwise ensuring that the project is moving to a successful close in a timely manner. Managers want to be accepted as members of the team and like to know exactly what is expected before they start new projects. As the ideas and tasks move back and forth between various team members, it is the Manager who will make sure that no one "drops the ball". Managers will have high level of interaction with all members of the team. They are considerate to people around them and will do their best to make the environment pleasing for others. They do not like confrontation but will handle it. They are conscientious and persuade others through a combination of logic and emotion. Managers are equipped with the ability to act as a dominant leader if their parameters of authority requires them to do so.

Key Value of Manager to TEAM

The Manager has the ability to clarify where and when ideas and concepts under development need to be moved from one member of the team to another. Their skill set allows them to move into the role of Theorist, Analyser or Strategist when necessary, and they can function in that role for a period of time. Their real strength is the ability to see things from a perspective of one of the team members and help another member of the team to understand the concept from their own perspective, acting as a sort of "conceptual translator" for the team.

Core Strengths of Manager

Managers are always considered when a leader is needed to move a project forward. They are able to communicate well with a large number of individuals, and also have the ability to delegate. Their attention to details and inner drive causes others to respect them, and to value their inputs into situations. Their keen ability to relate to others acts as a cohesive bond within the team, developing a strength and resiliency that adds depth.

Potential Limitations of Manager

The manager may appear distant at times, especially when focused on solving a problem. While sometimes seeming a bit aggressive, their fairness and people skills soon have others remembering that they want the best for all involved.

Strategist

The Strategist is the member of the team who identifies new concepts and ideas in their early stages, and develops the strategy behind their implementation. Strategists have an intrinsic grasp of how to market concepts and how to appeal to a broad range of individuals. They tend to be very task oriented but enjoy people as well. Strategists are often very good at recruiting; they tend to be friendly and outgoing, but also like to see tasks done properly. They influence others with excellent people skills and with the ability to reason and be logical. Strategists are not afraid to stand up and take charge if necessary. They are not bystanders but are constantly involved in some aspect of the project.

Strategists combine their previous experience with their knowledge of people to develop creative ways of getting the most benefit from a project or idea. The ability to simplify an idea or process is a key strength of Strategist. They will interact exceptionally well with Theorists, Managers and Analysers as they create their plans.

Key Value of Strategist to TEAM

The Strategist is a highly-creative problem solver with an inherent ability to compare and contrast a large number of ideas to determine their long-time implications. Frequently powerful communicators, they tend to be excellent encouragers and strong leaders. Strategists motivate others to achieve, drawing out the best in other team members. Their ability to explain things clearly and concisely makes them convincing spokespersons. They are powerful negotiators, and are able to make very accurate assessments of situations.

Core Strengths of Strategist

The strategist is perceived by most members of the team as great leaders, well-spoken and decisive. They naturally command the respect and attention of others. People follow them because of their charisma and enthusiasm. While Strategists may sometimes seem a bit aggressive, their fairness and people skills keep communications flowing.

Potential Limitations of Strategist

The Strategist may seem domineering and cool, sometimes losing sight of the people and focusing on the task. Strategists want others involved in their projects, but may forget about what others want. They need to listen more and think about what others around them may need. Strategists sometimes appear inconsistent or flighty due to their tendency to move rapidly from one concept to another, but it is precisely this rapid movement that allows them to consider the strategic implications of a given scenario. They need to learn to listen to people around them instead of always thinking about what they are going to say.

8.1.5 Exercise Five: Personal Values Analysis

You are about to embark on an exciting journey through the world of discovering your personal values.

Have you ever wondered why you respond differently to certain life experiences than others around you? It is because you operate on a system of values or invisible motivators that are unique to you! Value styles determine your perception of the world around you. They affect the choices you make, friends you choose, the career you pursue, your leisure activities, and even the words you say, in short, values determine how you live your life and all this is linked to your life purpose.

Conflicts often arise when we interact with an individual or group whose values clash with our own. We may not understand why people question our thoughts, decisions, opinions, actions, beliefs and attitudes. Without a proper understanding of differing value styles, this misunderstanding can cause us to build a wall around ourselves. If taken to the extreme, we may become fearful of interacting with people who do not perceive the world exactly as we do, or perhaps, we will continue to interact but never attain new levels of personal growth. The main reason for a lack of personal growth is due to an unwillingness to understand and accept others' point of view.

The Values Profile [9] is designed to help you discover your *"personal"* values style. Once this discovery is made, you can grow to understand and appreciate the differences in others. This understanding can become the foundation for building better relationships with the people in your life. Your values contribute to your unique behavior and have a direct relationship with your unique life purpose

[152]

The values system assessment is based on the forty statements listed below. Do not attempt to respond to these statements directly from this book. Instead I developed an online version which is available on website www.team6.co.za.

You can follow these steps to confirm your Values profile:

- Browse website www.team6.co.za
- Highlight "Leadership" from the main menu.
- Click "PRASI model" from the menu.
- Click "Values" from the diagram.

After completing all the statements on the website, the online version will respond with a specific description that applies to your own life. While answering these questions online, we ask that you remain completely honest and open-minded. This request is made for your own benefit. It is my desire that the Values Profile will enhance your ability to communicate and effectively interact with that personal and professional life while knowing quite well what your preferences are.

1 I am somewhat apprehensive of change and prefer to stick with the "tried and true" or what has worked in the past.

2 I "size up" people and situations based on my inner feelings.

3 I enjoyed situation that test my abilities and strength without restricting my personal freedom.

4 I enjoy bringing people and ideas together to achieve balance harmony.

5 I display strong loyalty and faithfulness towards the principles and concepts in which I believe.

6 I consider the wants, needs, and rights of others to be important

7 I prefer to exert influence over situations and environments in which I have placed myself.

8 I try not to pre-judge people places or things. I strive to remain open minded without losing my inner balance.

9 Moral character, integrity, and honesty are important to me.

10 I approach others in an open and non-threatening manner.

[154]

11 I prefer to set my own priorities rather than being influenced by others or what is popular.

12 I seek to make my words conform to reality, and reality conforms to my words.

13 I believe, if you don't stand for something you will fall for anything.

14 I always give my best effort to those areas that provide personal satisfaction.

15 I have a strong inner drive to gain recognition and sense of wellbeing by doing things my own way.

16 I have deep-rooted concern for the welfare of others, sometimes to my own detriment.

17 I place a higher priority on meeting deadlines and keeping promises .My word is my bond.

18 I want others to be pleased with my empathy, concern and warmth towards them

19 I perceive things to be a certain way and strive to make situations conform to my personal goals.

20 I am determined to stick to the things I believe in, but I attempt to maintain flexibility in an effort to achieve harmony.

21 I approach many systems and problems from a logical rather than emotional perspective.

22 I strive to establish rapport with others by being considerate to their views and feelings.

23 I easily recognize opportunities that will benefit me and move swiftly to capitalize on them.

24 I try to see the positive possibilities in all people and things.

25 I feel it is important to build and maintain the trust of others. Having a good reputation is of utmost importance to me.

26 I have a strong sense of fair play. However; I dislike situations that I find restrictive to my self-expression.

27 I have a quick and seek creative solutions that will better satisfy my objectives.

28 I feel I have gained and apply a good bit of wisdom from my experiences in life.

29 I remain very loyal once I have decided to align myself with an idea organization or process.

30 I will set my personal desires to maintain harmony, if my goals a met by doing so.

31 I strive to accomplish goals that will enhance my emotional and psychological satisfaction.

32 I enjoy sharing and combining ideas with others to improve productivity and quality.

33 I want to attain goals, see things through, play by the rules, and be recognized by my contributions.

34 I desire situations which consistently provide me with a feeling of inner peace.

35 I will adjust circumstances so I can enhance my feelings of accomplishment of well-being. "You only go around once, so make more of it".

36 I respond well to others and they react favorably to me. I treat everyone with respect and dignity.

37 I prefer for things to remain steady, constant and unchanged. No surprises please!

38 I strive and search for harmony in all things, tangible and intangible, and in all those accomplishments which provide personal fulfillment.

39 I enjoy testing my performance against others or an established standard. I also want to set my own standards.

40 I enjoy performing tasks and sharing performance with others

Listed and described below are four categories of the values system. Any one of these four will apply to your life depending on your response to the online questionnaire.

Loyalty

General Characteristics...

The characteristics of individuals with a high loyalty values style are:

- Focusing on people working together for the greater good.

- Protecting from challenging situations by responsible living and pooling together.

- Avoiding the loss of social respect from others.

- Following the proper and correct way of doing things in accordance with established rules and authority

- Conforming to traditional patterns through personal commitments and promises.

Potential Limitations...

The more energy expended towards Loyalty, the greater the chance of becoming locked into a pattern of thinking

Overview

[158]

- Focus: On traditions

- Outlook: recognizes established authority

- Goal: Responsible living

- Fear: Loss of social respect/disloyalty

- Work style: Meaningful involvement

Equality

General Characteristics...

The characteristics of individuals with high Equality value styles are:

- Focusing on respecting the individuality of others as well as self.

- Respecting individual beliefs.

- Searching for personal fulfillment and making opportunities for meaningful communication with others.

- Avoiding inner conflicts.

Potential Limitations....

The more energy expended towards Equality, the greater the chance of losing track of day-to-day responsibilities.

Overview...

- Focus: Self-expression

- Outlook: seeks friendly relationships with the freedom to be themselves

- Goal: Self-assertion and happiness

- Fear: Inner conflict/inequality

- Work style: socially acceptable individual

Personal Freedom

General Characteristics...

The characteristics of individuals with a high personal freedom values style are:

- Challenging or questioning the existing systems, rules, standards and procedures in order to increase the boundaries of personal freedom.

- Seeking self-preservation and satisfaction through the accomplishments of personal goals.

- Preventing the loss of personal wellbeing.

- Expressing energy through creative, untested and nonconventional ideas.

Potential Limitations….

The more energy expended towards Personal Freedom, the greater the chance of win/lose situations developing.

Overview…

- Focus: Self-fulfillment

- Outlook: seeks personal goals and aspirations

- Goal: Self-satisfaction

- Fear: Loss of personal well-being

- Work style: Self-expressed individuality

Justice

General Characteristics...

The Characteristics of individuals with a high justice value style are;

- Finding fulfillment through meaningful relationships and seeking fair and workable solutions.

- Bettering conditions of the environment for the common good, even at their own personal expense, as long as everyone will benefit.

- Avoiding situation that are unjust or conflicting with a senses of inner honesty.

- Improving the present quality of life even though the number of personal benefits may be decreased.

Potential Limitations

The more energy expended towards Justice, the greater the chance of overextending personal energies and personal resources.

Overview…

- Focus: Inner honesty.

- Outlook: Seeks personal acceptance with others for the common good.

- Goal: Acceptance into the group.

- Fear: Lack of personal harmony and injustice.

- Work style: Personal involvement.

Chapter 9

Challenges

"Many are tribulations of the righteous"

Life

9 Challenges in Finding Life Purpose

The toughest person to face is yourself. If we look at ourselves in the mirror in the morning by afternoon we would have forgotten how we look like and may need to check in the mirror again. This is the reality of man

The real test of a man's courage is the ability to face and change self. We don't like to face issues because many times facing an issue means we have to face our own selves, and seeing our shortcomings is not easy, much less comfortable. It is easier to blame everyone else for everything than to introspect and come up with self-management resolutions. Most people would prefer to make themselves victims of everyone and everything else. It is because of someone else that they are depressed. They could not do this and that because of so and so, and their day was horrible because of what so and so said or did. The thing is we can decide to manage ourselves internally, or let someone or something else manage us externally, which makes us subject to changing circumstances and whims of other people. We need to learn to wall ourselves in so that we only allow what we want in and out of our gates – this is what it means to rule over your spirit: managing yourself. The worst thing is for one to try and manage others when they cannot manage self, and sometimes the more the desire to manage others the greater the indication of lack of self-management. Life needs to have boundaries – to have bounds for self as well as for others, so we can keep them – and us – from getting out of bounds. And once the boundaries are defined, the greatest challenge is to respect boundaries you made for yourself, by yourself, and with only yourself to account to. Once we master this, we can master anything, because what we are has much less to do with our environment than it has to do with who we are. The truth of the matter is that we too often disrespect ourselves much more than others disrespect us.

Are you operating out of bounds?

Chapter 10

Examples

"It is finished"

Life

10 Examples of Purposeful Lives

In all cases, people who live their lives on purpose always leave behind them a long legacy. They make history, and I mean good history. They do not only become successful but they become very great. They are always a source of inspiration to several generations that come after them. Strangely enough there is very little mention of money and wealth when making reference to life purpose. It's always about impact on human lives and overcoming the seemingly impossible. At the same time there is no room for poverty when it comes to a life that is lived on purpose. Also to strengthen the cause of Purpose, people who identify their life purpose are prepared to die for their life purpose.

Below are examples of such people from both religious and secular world. I included Jesus Christ's examples as these are most crisp and the best to make reference to. Where possible, I have also explained what it is that defines their purpose

[170]

statements as well as what they did to achieve that purpose. The list is endless therefore I have picked only on a few for illustration. I included a component of the spiritual gift at work given that all great characters (in the scriptures for example), were all operating under the influence of the Spirit of the Lord.

Jesus Christ	Description
Gift(s)	A combination of all special abilities. His prominent gifts that He left behind for the running of the church are most commonly referred to as the five-fold Ministry gifts. They are the gifts of Teaching, Prophesy, Apostleship, Evangelism and Pastoring.
Purpose	To save mankind from sin. All of Jesus Christ's teachings, healing, prophesy and other activities were focused on liberating man from bondage of

sin. Jesus Christ was killed for this purpose but His works are still changing lives today and forever.

Martin Luther	Description
Gift(s)	Spiritual ability to serve
Purpose	To promote civil rights for blacks

Mother Theresa	Description
Gift(s)	Spiritual aptitude of Mercy
Purpose	To care for the poor

Nelson Mandela	Description
Gift(s)	Servant Leadership
Purpose	To abolish human oppression by another

Chapter 11

Fulfilment

"Faith without action is dead"

Life

11 How to Fulfil Your Life Purpose

Once you confirm your life purpose it is not a stage to then sit back and relax, it is actually a time to take massive action. You need both faith and commitment. You cannot just wait around for your possibilities to take place on their own. Knowing your purpose makes you like a co-creator. A co-creator of possibility knows better than to wait and let circumstance dictate what is possible and what is not. You must be intentional in making things happen. Performance can only be affected by one thing: **Action**. If there is no action, there will be no performance; the less action, the less performance. Non-performance equals non-action. Your purpose is there to fuel you up into taking this action.

Most people like to talk about action, without actually carrying out any. Successful people are different from ordinary people because they take action. High performers become successful while those who limit their performance become mediocre. Your actions ultimately reveal who you are being in your life.

Success is not exclusive to some people. However, it is only the people who are willing to make things happen that can truly perform their lives. Why can some people act, while others can't? It's because of their stand. If their stand touches, moves, and inspires them into action, then they will certainly be propelled into action.

Brothers and Sisters I do not want you to remain ignorant of the fact that life is a journey, a journey which is consistently measured against time. And as far as we know it, time is always moving. Therefore fulfillment of life purpose means that your activities are on a parallel or same journey with the time that is made available to you.

Talking of a journey, let us look at a simple illustration of an ordinary journey that one can undertake in everyday life. You are sitting now in city A and you want to go on a journey to city B which is say sixty kilometers away.

Firstly for this journey to take place there must be a reason why you want to embark on this journey.

There has to be a driving motive for you to set out on this journey. That driving motive or that reason for embarking on this journey is what we call PURPOSE.

Now before you start on this journey there are a couple of questions that will come into mind and these include:

a) What is the reason for you to decide on going to city B- The answer to this represents purpose.

b) When you get to city B, what is it that you are going to do in that city B- The answer to this represents a mission.

c) What is it that you want to achieve before you leave city B and return to city A- The answer to this represents an objective or goal.

d) What are the activities that you want to carry out in order to achieve your objectives while in city B- The answer to this represents a plan.

e) How will you carry out these activities or these tasks while you are in city B- The answer to this represents a strategy.

f) Whom will you need to assist you to carry out the tasks or activities in city B- The answer to this represents team building?

g) How do you plan to get to city B? What means of transport is most suitable- The answer to this represents resource requirements.

By addressing the above questions it means you will create a clear picture in your mind of the outcome of this journey before you set out to travel. This illustration provides a strategic plan to your journey and the same approach applies to the journey of your life as well. The next sub-section provides more detail on the answers provided above.

11.1　Crafting a Life Vision Statement

By definition, vision is an end-state of achievement after all the work has been done successfully. This end-state picture can be viewed at as many years from now. As part of creating a vision you can actually describe how you want your life to be fifteen years from today. Now take that description and work on it backwards breaking it down into smaller pieces of achievement up to today. Then in real life start by working on that smallest piece today and reverse the process. Vision is actually created in the imagination and described prior to or during undertaking of the planned work.

When you go to bed and close your eyes, vision is what you start to see with your inner eyes. The vision we are referring to is not the normal things that you see with your eyes open; vision is actually the picture that you see with your spiritual or inner eyes. This end-state picture can be representing an ideal which is likely to manifest maybe five to twenty years from now. "What you see is what you get"

As I coach lives on a daily basis, the result is that I connect people with their purpose. Their lives then become orderly, successful and fulfilled. As I continue coaching lives, the lives of more and more people become orderly, successful and fulfilled. Therefore what I foresee in years to come are orderly, successful, prosperous and fulfilled lives everywhere in Africa.

I can therefore conclude that my vision is, to see "successful and prosperous lives everywhere in Africa, more so with entrepreneurs".

11.2   Crafting a Life Mission Statement

Mission is your assignment here on Earth. It is the set of activities that you are assigned to do in your life for others. In other instances it is referred to as your main task in life. This is linked to what Jesus referred to in Matthew 16 verse 24 [1] when He said "Whoever wants to be my disciple must deny themselves and take up their cross and follow me". The cross is the burden you carry in life and you are the person assigned by God to deal with that burden. Your mission also defines the set of challenges you are presented with in life. You are then called by God to deal with these challenges.

Your mission gives meaning to your life. Your mission links to your very reason for existence.

You are not alone in this search. This mission is also looking for you. It wants to be fulfilled by you and by nobody else. It is your personal

[180]

mission. Nobody else is equipped to do it for you. Your mission will keep haunting you until you take it seriously and start implementing it.

Going against your mission is going against yourself. This is the same as ignoring the call of your soul, as ignoring your strongest desires, as signing a contract for eternal discontent... The book of Jonah 1 verses 16-17 [2] confirms it all. "Then the men feared the LORD greatly and they offered a sacrifice to the LORD and made vows. And the LORD appointed a great fish to swallow Jonah and Jonah was in the stomach of the fish three days and three nights". This incident happened when Jonah was trying to escape from his mission.

You cannot escape your mission. One day you will have to start dedicating yourself to it.

Has this day come for you now? After all, you are reading these lines which show your honest desire to start looking for the deeper meaning of your being.

Let us look at a very clear example, which is the mission statement of Jesus Christ whose mission was to deliver people from bondage of sin. As mentioned in Luke 4 verse 18 [1] Jesus Christ used the following methods to carry out His mission:

- Preaching good news to the poor
- Proclaiming freedom to prisoners
- Healing the sick
- Saving the lost

Throughout the New Testament Scriptures we see that Jesus Christ was delivering people on a daily basis using the above methods. Delivering people is the cross that Jesus Christ was carrying, and when He got nailed to that cross He declared that it is finished. In other words He had accomplished His mission and made sure that His purpose goes through future generations forever.

Mission always describes what it is that you get out of your house to do on a daily basis for people. It also describes the target market to which you do those things. In comparison to Jesus's mission statement I also developed my own mission statement and methods as follows:

Mission statement is:

"to help entrepreneurs clarify their life purpose so they can use it in developing strategies for their businesses and management of their projects".

How I achieve this is by the following:

- Giving direction to the lost
- Bringing hope to the perishing
- Inspiring the disillusioned

You can clearly see that the problems that I solve are among the LPD. This mission is the "cross" that I carry throughout the rest of my life. I accomplish this mission through various means as per my method statement and these various means include:

- Print and electronic life management publications, where I write and publish books like this one as well as use online tools to assist people to manage and bring order and clarity to their lives.

- Talk shows and motivational presentations where I inspire those who have lost hope and are disillusioned.

- One-on-one or group life coaching sessions where I assist people to clarify their life purpose and align it with strategies for their lives and lives of their businesses.

I do this for both personal life and business life, remembering that business is an entity that has its own life from conception, birth, growth, stability, decline and eventually death.

In summary, mission is the answer to the following question: When I start the day everyday what is it that I am going out there to do for people? How do I do it? How well do I do it? And to which group of people do I do it?

Below are examples. The table below is a carryover from the one in section 10, only that the description of life mission has been added to each of the examples.

Jesus Christ	Description
Gift(s)	A combination of all special abilities. His prominent gifts that He left behind for the running of the church are most commonly referred to as the five-fold Ministry gifts. They are the gifts of Teaching, Prophesy, Apostleship, Evangelism and Pastoring
Purpose	To save mankind from sin. All of Jesus Christ's teachings, healing, prophesy and other activities were focused on liberating man from bondage of

sin. Jesus Christ was killed for this purpose but His works are still changing lives today and forever.

Mission	To deliver people from bondage by preaching good news to the poor, healing the sick, saving the lost and proclaiming freedom for prisoners

Martin Luther .	Description
Gift(s)	Spiritual ability to serve
Purpose	To promote civil rights for blacks
Mission	To free blacks from oppression by preaching civil rights and teaching economic and political justice to Americans

Mother Theresa	Description
Gift(s)	Spiritual aptitude of Mercy
Purpose	To care for the poor

Mission	To care for the poor by providing food and shelter

Nelson Mandela

	Description
Gift(s)	Servant Leadership
Purpose	To abolish human oppression by another
Mission	To eliminate human oppression by promoting justice and equal rights

11.3   Crafting a Life Strategy

Strategy is the positioning for a success.

Strategy answers the questions, "what should you do and how should you position yourself in order to continue being fruitful as you aim to achieve your life vision as you operate in your area of purpose?"

Often in business circles you will hear several of these terms thrown around without a clear definition. You will hear people talk of having a mission statement or a vision statement. Rarely do you hear them talk about having, what I believe is the most important thing, a personal or corporate purpose statement which should be the beacon to all plans. However, we have always encouraged people to develop some form of a life strategy so they have something to look forward to, and, at the same time, set productive goals that have meaning and substance.

A life without some life strategy is like a boat without a rudder. Your boat will definitely get you somewhere due to the forces of wind and water currents, but where you end up may not be where you want to go.

For that reason, it is important to give your life some direction to end up where you want to be in life in the future.

Bear in mind that you do not have to give up spontaneity or the natural evolution of your life to embrace a life strategy even twenty years into the future. It is equally important to be open to all possibilities in your life so that you do not overlook opportunities that might come to you.

You will discover that when you have a life strategy that has a fifteen to twenty year horizon you will be continually refining your life strategy as you gain more knowledge and experience in your life. Additionally, you will also learn to fine-tune opportunities as they present themselves, which further enhances the fulfilment of your life strategy.

Consider a long-range life strategy as a chart of your future, which has elasticity so that you can tweak it from time to time to perfect its outcome.

Conversely, you should build your life strategy on a solid foundation of clear life-goals such as self-reliance, financial self-sufficiency, and entrepreneurship.

Does your life strategy change? Yes, it certainly does. The biggest change is that you now have to extend your retirement age to sixty or more instead of fifty. Then again, based on all of the knowledge, valuable contacts, and business savvy you have acquired in your life thus far you might be able to shorten the time horizon to your goal.

More often than not that is exactly what happens with entrepreneurs who encounter a major setback, they come back even stronger. As a result, the life-strategy goal of retiring a multi-millionaire does not change, only the timeline changes.

Some important components of a strategy are called the SWOT analysis. SWOT is an acronym for Strengths, Weaknesses, Opportunities and Threats. You have to critically analyse each of these components in your own individual or business life. Strengthen your strong areas, identify and capture new opportunities, develop mitigations for risks that lie ahead and also find help to support you in areas where you are weak. This applies to both individual lives and business lives.

Clearly, developing a life strategy makes a lot of sense and can be useful to just about anyone. The diagram in fig 2 below helps you to understand some very important areas that constitute a strategy.

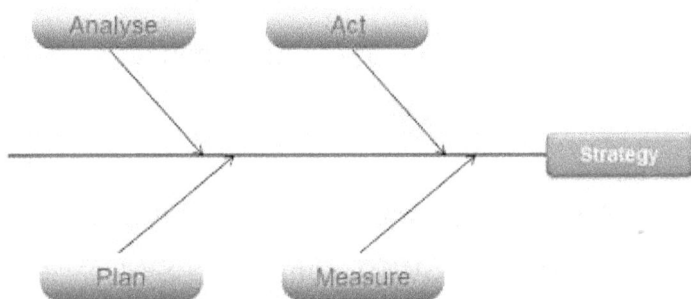

Fig 2 - A strategy model

Some guidelines in the development of a strategy:

S – Stick to the plan

T- Think through it

R – Risk versus rewards

A – Awareness

T – Talk it out and share with others

E – Evaluate each step

G – Grow people, empowerment

Y – Yes I can attitude

DONT's

- Don't make unrealistic assumptions
- Don't underestimate difficulties
- Don't underestimate effort

11.4   Setting Goals

Goals are your intended achievements in a fairly long term. An example of a goal could be "to become a millionaire in 3 years."

My goal for the next six months is to publish a second life purpose book for which I already have a title.

11.5   Setting Objectives

Objectives are smaller and more manageable targets that are planned to be delivered within short timeframes. We may refer to these short term objectives as "deliverables." These deliverables put together will contribute to the achievements of your longer term goals. An example could be "to buy and sell products and make a profit of $1000 in one month."

In managerial terms, objectives are supposed to comply with the acronym "SMART". This means that the objective when planned should be Stretching, Measurable, Achievable, and Realistic and have a Timeframe attached to it.

An example of an objective in my case is to research and compile a contents page for my second book in the next two weeks.

11.6 Developing a Life Plan

A plan is like a roadmap that shows implementation activities that are required to achieve objectives. Common components of a plan are the following:

- Description of activity

- Who will carry out the activity

- How much time will the activity require

- How much time will it take to achieve the overall set of activities

11.7 Bearing Fruit

The first commandment by God to mankind is to bear fruit. He says in Genesis 1 verse 28 [2] "Be fruitful, and multiply and replenish the Earth and subdue it: and have dominion over the fish of the sea, and over the fowl of the air and every little thing that moves over the Earth"

Also in John 15 verse 2 [2] Jesus says "And every one that bears fruit, He prunes..." It is so that it may bring forth more fruit.

The worst thing that can ever happen to someone is to think that they have arrived. It is a sad day when you think you know everything. There should always be room for growth and improvement, and if not, God will ensure that He forces it upon you. It's not the little dying and withering trees that are pruned; it's the healthy trees that are even bearing fruit that the vinedresser tends to give special attention to, and helps with a little pruning. Some of the challenges we experience have nothing to do with our having sinned or anything like that; they have to do with the pruning process that we all go through to increase our fruit-bearing

Churches also go through pruning, where they shrink in order that they may grow. If you're flourishing, and bearing good fruit, get ready for pruning. Yes, it will hurt, and you will seem to be losing some of the fruit-bearing branches, but the vinedresser knows exactly what He is doing, because He knows you will be more productive with less than with more. It's a lesson we are not very keen on in our numbers-based success measurement. It's good to the eye to see all the branches and leaves around, looking good and in abundance, and that is where we get to sometimes. We have the numbers, and some strong-looking, leafy branches, but it is then, just when you think you should be left alone, that God comes and brings more pruning. It is because God does not want you to be just good; He wants you to do better, and when you do better, He will not rest until you are the best.

Have you lost some branches lately? With them you were good, but you will be better without them and bearing much fruit.

11.8   Handling Issues and Blockages

Excuses – "But they all alike began to make excuses" Luke 14:18 [1]

Sports haters in high school had a very smart way of keeping away from sports: they simply obtained a fake doctor's medical excuse to feign sickness. That's exactly what excuses do: they "feign illness" to keep us from doing what we should be doing. You see, you may hide behind your excuses, but you remain bound by them, no matter how good, valid or understandable they are. They are still excuses, and have no power to change your circumstance. All they just do is pacify you and kill your desire to change or do something about your situation – because you have an excuse not to. You may have a great and valid excuse for stinking breath, but your breath is still stinking even after eloquently outlying the excuse and having got everyone to agree and feel sorry for you. Everyone may understand what led to your dire poverty, but your plate is still empty until you get rid of the excuse and do something about your situation

There are people who had daunting situations in their lives; they overcome those the moment they refused to use those circumstances as excuses. Truth of the matter is, most people are just plain liars trying to use their excuse to cover up for their unwillingness to do the work, or too lazy to do something to change their situations. When you look at some of the amazing things done by disabled people, you may wonder what it is that makes able-bodied people do less. Their excuses make their ability a disability.

Excuses are just clutches upon which your failure leans. Get rid of excuses, and act on changing your life. After all, God expects and accepts no excuses.

What is your excuse? Rather have faith and not doubt in your actions...."Faith by itself, if it is not accompanied by action, is dead" James 2 verse 17 [1].

Do not use lack of money as an excuse. There is a saying that money is not a problem— "Empty pockets never held anyone back. Only empty heads and empty hearts can do that." - Norman Vincent Peale [10]. So do not use money as an excuse for not pursuing your purpose. Once you are aligned with your purpose money will naturally get attracted to you.

Do not let the prosperity of wicked people distract you. In Jeremiah 12 verses 1-4 the Prophet was complaining about how unrighteous and wicked people prosper, whereas the Prophet himself was not prospering, even though he was upright and righteous. God replied in Jeremiah 12 verse 5 [1] "If you have raced with men on foot and they

[201]

have worn you out, how can you compete with horses? If you stumble in a safe country, how will you manage in the thickets by Jordan?" This verse provides lots of encouragement in that God allows you a delay so as to prepare you for greater things that are beyond the ordinary.

Do not allow ignorance to hinder you. Reading:* Jeremiah 33-34, Luke 24, Psalm 55, and Proverbs 14 the Lord says: "Call to me and I will answer you and tell you great and unsearchable things you do not know" (Jeremiah 3 verse 33) [1]. Ignorance is not bliss, especially when it has to do with spiritual things.

It happens because we do not heed the call to talk to God. Not everyone with greatly exciting secrets wants to share them, but our Heavenly Father has openly told us to call for the secrets, and He will happily show us. Many Christians wander in a maze of perplexity, but help is only a call away. God is alive; He hears, and answers and shows. He will show you the secrets to solving personal issues, and dealing with situations. He will show you wonderful things that are not common to everyone, only to those who ask Him.

Like the good old song says, you can dial heaven any time. The lines are never busy; you're never put on hold. You will never be told that He's out of the office, gone on a journey, or that He is currently attending to someone else nor do the lines cut off before you finish your conversation. No, you won't get a voice recording either. And what's best, the Receptionist Himself is able to help you, because He was once a man and understands how you feel, so He won't be telling you to try the next help centre, or saying they don't "deal with such issues".

Do you have some marvellous things you don't know and would like to know about in your life right now? What are you waiting for? Talk to God about them

Chapter 12

Inspiration

"The vision awaits its appointed time"

Life

12 Inspiration and Motivation

12.1 God's Waiting Room

Remember that purpose identification is not an event but it is a process. At certain stages of the process it will appear as if there actually is neither progress in life nor in the identification of purpose. We call this stage "being in God's waiting room". Do not turn a blind eye to activities during these stages. Whatever you will be doing will be adding to the support system of your life purpose.

Do not be discouraged by delays or if you do not seem to find your purpose or your vision, for in Habakkuk 2 [1] the Lord says: "Write the vision and make it plain on tablets so he may run who reads it. For still the vision awaits its appointed time; it hastens to the end- it will not lie. If it seems slow wait for it; it will surely come and it will not delay".

[206]

12.2 Trust in God

"Cursed is the man who trusts in man, and makes flesh his arm." (Jeremiah 17:5) [2]

You drop your well-written business proposal into the Christian businessman's inbox, expecting him, as a brother, to obviously pull the trigger, work a few wonders and make sure you get the funding you need – simple as that. He has the clout to do it for you if he wanted to. But it's the months that elapse, or the not-so-encouraging response from his office, that begins to bring the disillusionment, with feelings of being betrayed and let down. It is a blessing to have those among us to whom God has entrusted resources and means whereby they may help the body of Christ.

However, sometimes they fall under great pressure from people who expect them to work wonders and play God. When you have a business, everyone expects you to give them a job, or violate company procedures to accommodate them. Don't put pressure on man. Man is not your source.

At best he will be used by God to help your situation. When you look up to men, you elevate that man to be your source, bringing a curse upon yourself. Engage man as much as possible, but at the end of the day commit the outcome to the LORD.

Put your trust in God, and not in man. God is responsible for your life, not the banker or the businesswoman in the church. Free man from playing God because man will fail you, and there should be nothing unusual about that. Man is expected and disposed to fail. But God is not. So trust in the one who will not fail, and when man fails you, you will understand it, and save yourself from disappointment and heartbreak. Take up your case with God, not the man whom you expected to provide.

[208]

Because if God will not have you get the job, or the capital, the businessperson will not be able to give it to you even if he wanted to. Don't hate. He's only human, with limited power and influence. Let your trust be in God, not man.

12.3 God's Encouragement

If fear is holding you back then be reminded that fear stands for_False Evidence Appearing Real.

"There is no fear in love, but perfect love casts out fear, because fear has torment. He who fears has not been perfected in love." (1 John 4 verse 18)

The reason God can totally love is because He is totally fearless. Love cannot coexist with fear, and vice-versa. One can only love to the extent they are liberated from fear. When you feel totally loved, you will be totally secure. Love requires security, and the less secure we are, the less able we are to love or receive love. Fear is the absence of love. This is why we cannot love like God can: we're full of fear. This fear is present because we avoid abuse, being taken advantage of and meeting with the past so we try to protect ourselves, refusing to be vulnerable, but love cannot exist without vulnerability. When women fight Biblical submission to their husbands, it is not because they're imagining what a loving husband can do with a totally submitting wife. Instead, fearful, they cannot submit, because they feel they have to protect themselves. Until they are able to transcend fear –either through the manifestation of the husband's love, or their own dealing with fear - they live less-than-satisfactory relationships where they can never be truly submissive. That is the reason people who love their job can keep time much better than those who are afraid of being fired. That is because love energises and motivates, but fear paralyses and torments. Any Christian who will follow God for fear of going to hell is probably going there already, because the fear of hell can bring you into the Kingdom of God, but it cannot keep you in it. To remain saved requires understanding, believing, receiving and reciprocating the love of God, because love is the language that God speaks.

12.4 Some Motivation

The day you consider yourself to have arrived is the day you are finished. The day you stop growing, you are dying. The world is moving forward, and those people who will continuously develop themselves will remain relevant. There is much more to know than you know already, and there is much more of God to explore. You might have done exploits thus far, but who says you cannot do more? While you are still on the planet, there is still work for you to do. Past testimonies are great, but we need recent, current things that God is doing in your life. It is not enough to know what God did; we need to know what He is doing now. It is not enough to know what God said; you need to know what He is saying now. You have to keep growing in your faith, in maturity and in spirit. If you were leading two people, see if you can lead three. Do not be satisfied and become complacent because of your achievements. Go on, get hold of that which Christ has got hold for you. There is a reason why you are still in this world. You only retire from growing when you die. Get to know God more, touch more people, save more, heal more, and do more. Thank God for what He has done with and through you, but even more for what He is yet to do. Lay hold of the promise. You are not there yet. God has greater, dizzier heights He wants to take you to. Do not settle for an anthill when you could scale a mountain. Do not settle for good when you could get better

Chapter 13

FAQs

"If any of you lacks wisdom, let them ask"

Life

13 Frequently Asked Questions

Q Why are some people seemingly born with a lot of success e.g. Bill Gates, Tiger Woods etc.:

A Because of His sovereignty, the Lord can bless whom He wants to bless and curse whom He wants to curse. Sometimes the Lord blesses a person because He wants to use that specific person as an example for something that the Lord wants to demonstrate among people on Earth. Sometimes historical generations may have sinned against God and as a result He may also choose to punish future generations for those historical sins. We cannot choose whom God should bless. God is sovereign and does as He wills and according to His ways that are above our ways as humans.

Q Can one's purpose change?

A No. You can have many expressions of purpose but the essence of who you are remains the

[216]

same. At a basic level my purpose is to create order in lives of people. Whatever my role, I find the chaos and bring the order. I do this when I write, speak, consult, travel, administrate and coach. I have done this as a project management consultant, managing director, life coach, mentor and author. I have brought order out of chaos in many different ways, but my purpose always stays the same.

Q Can one have more than one purpose?

A No. You can have many expressions of that purpose but still only one purpose. It helps if you make the distinction between role and purpose. My role as a father has changed over the years from when my children were small to now that they are adults. I also had a role as an electrical engineer, which I fulfilled for a number of years, but no longer do. Yet my essence that enables me to create order never changes, no matter what role I play at different stages of my life.

Q What advice do you have for a husband and wife pursuing purpose?

A I seldom see one person's purpose defined in terms of another, unless there is a severe disability or handicap that necessitates a spouse, sibling, or parent to devote much time to the care of their partner or child. In other words, a wife's purpose isn't to help her husband or raise her children. A woman has purpose before she marries or has children and will have purpose long after the children are gone or her husband departs this life.

Most marriages try to create unity by maintaining uniformity. My advice to any couple is to find your individual purpose and then creatively work to see how both parties can find fulfilment. It takes faith and effort, but it can be done [11]

Q What about children? How old should they be when you talk to them about purpose?

A You start talking about purpose as early as possible and especially when it seems that God is talking to your young person about purpose. Also, please don't spend too much time pressuring your children to choose a career path. Help them identify and get comfortable with their strengths and weaknesses and urge them to pursue what they love, regardless of what the employment prospects look like. I am not saying they won't need a job, but to direct them into something from which they will earn income but for which they have no passion, is a ticket to trouble in the long run. They will burn out and be frustrated. The sooner you can talk about purpose, the better [11]

Q I thought I was to do anything God wanted me to do. Why should I search for purpose?

A While it sounds noble to say, "I'll do whatever you want, Lord," it is actually a cop-out and an attempt to avoid knowing the specific thing you were created to do. After all, you cannot be held accountable for what you don't know. Yet that thinking creates a passive attitude that puts the burden of action on God; He must show you what to do rather than you discovering what He wants you to do. Passive people usually don't find purpose. Those who actively seek it find it and they find not only what they are to do, but also what they are not to do. [11]

Q Is there any difference between mission, calling, vocation, destiny, vision and purpose?

A I chose purpose as the word to describe God's will for your life because it seemed to have the least "baggage" attached to it. It is a word that can be used in secular and spiritual settings and it is one with which all people seem comfortable. Some simple definitions below may help:

- Purpose: This is the reason for your being and existence representing God's will in your life.

- Mission: This is your personal assignment here on Earth.

- Vision: This is the picture of achievement in the long term as you carry out your assignment, mostly expressed in a number of years. A vision is something a person can possess unlike a calling which possesses a person. You can ignore a vision but never a calling.

- Calling: This is your specific role that is required to fulfil your given assignment e.g. Saul then named Paul in the Scriptures, was called to be an Apostle. Note here the difference with mission. Paul was "*called*" to be an Apostle for a special "*mission*" to preach the gospel to Gentiles. I am *"called"* to be a Life Coach with a *"mission"* to clarify life purpose of entrepreneurs.

- Vocation: This is your skilled profession, occupation or career e.g. an Accountant.

- Destiny: This is the predetermined course of your life.

- Strategy: This is a positioning for success especially considering the competition.

Q What is the difference between a gift and purpose?

A Your gifts are tools in your tool box that help you fulfil your purpose. A plumber's purpose isn't to wrench. The plumber carries a wrench to help him (or her) to plumb, so to speak. I write, but my writing is a gift that helps me create order in life by connecting people with their purpose. I am an experienced project manager, but that is a gift that I use to help people to plan and strategize as I link them with their purpose. Don't stop when you define your gifts. If you have a gift of music, ask what effect it has on others, what feedback you receive and why you love it as much as you do.

Q Why is my purpose so difficult to discover?

A It is hard to find because we have been conditioned to think in certain ways. First, we are often not comfortable talking about who we are. So when I ask someone what their purpose is, I may hear something like this: "Well, I sort of, maybe, sometimes enjoy doing this or that, not that I'm very good and I may be wrong." Then we have been taught to find a job and not work with what we love:

"I love to paint but everyone knows you can't make a living doing that, so I don't paint." Then we have been taught to be humble and to even deny that we do something well: "That was a wonderful dinner party!" Response: "Oh, it was nothing!" Plus, purpose is so second nature that we tend to look right past it, waiting for something more spiritual, more "unlike" us. I often hear two words when people get close to describing their purpose. Those two words are "just" and "only." People say, "I just listen to people" or "I only love to shop." We don't find purpose because of negative thinking [11]

Q What should I do once I discover my purpose?

A As outlined in Section 11 you have to move forward to fulfilment stage. God wants you to fulfil your purpose more than you do, so He will meet you more than halfway. The fulfilment of purpose will find you. That doesn't mean you don't have to get ready and improve. Work with God to clarify your vision and mission. Take lessons, read books, practice, go to places where your purpose is celebrated, talk to people, but don't feel like you have to do something. Rest in God and watch Him bring the problems to you for which you are the solution [11].

Q It all seems so complicated to me. Can you simplify the process?

A I can. It's all about doing what you love doing. Why would God give you a love to do something – and God has created you and is intimately acquainted with all your ways– and then not allow you to do it? Is God a tease? He is not! So find what gives you joy and do it as often as possible. If people pay you to do it, fine. If not, then do it when the kids are in bed or after your salaried job. Don't try to figure it out or rationalize it, just do it and let God lead you where you need to be, where you want to be – to a place where the joy of the Lord is your strength. Another simple piece of advice is for you to find something you enjoy doing for people and NOT getting paid for it. There lies your purpose.

Chapter 14

Self Help

"He gives you strength to make wealth"

Life

14 Tools to Help You

This book can be read and used in conjunction with website www.team6.co.za which contains a wide range of online tools and techniques that can be used in identification of life purpose as well crafting strategies for success especially for small to medium sized enterprises. The online tools are for free.

Chapter 15

The Journey

"Be fruitful and multiply"

Life

15 Enjoy the Journey

The journey is now clear, so be set for forward and fruitful movement in your life and enjoy all the personal success and prosperity that comes with it.

Chapter 16

Acknowledgements

"In everything give thanks"

Life

16 Acknowledgements

Dr. John Stanko

Dr. John Stanko is the President of Purpose Quest Incorporation in USA. I thank him for conducting my first one-on-one life purpose assessment in 2005. Since that time I never looked back on the subject of pursuing life purpose. Most of the QA content in this book comes from one of his books.

Celebration Church in Zimbabwe, Rhema Church and King of Glory Ministries in South Africa

I thank the above Churches for taking me through the journey of spiritual rebirth and providing the encouragement to pursue purpose in my life. Most of the religious content in this book is related to the teachings from these Churches.

A portion of the proceeds from this book will be donated to these Churches

Chapter 17

The Author

Life

17 About the Author

Paul Keta became a Management and Life Coach as a calling. He is a born again Christian and Christianity provided a strong background and motivation to becoming a Life Coach focusing on entrepreneurs and business leaders. Paul is a Management Professional certified by the Project Management Institute, Pennsylvania in USA and has extensive business and people management experience. This experience includes several years of managing projects in the Electrical Engineering and Information and Communication Technology fields for various large organizations in Africa. Paul is also an entrepreneur running a management consulting practice called Team Six Consultants, which provides leadership, strategic and project management services to small businesses in Africa. Team Six Consultants is accessible on www.team6.co.za.

Paul lives with his family and two daughters in Johannesburg, South Africa.

[234]

Paul's short profile:

- Purpose: To create order and growth in lives of emerging Entrepreneurs

- Calling: To be a Life and Management Coach

- Mission: To help entrepreneurs clarify their life purpose and link it to strategies of their businesses

- Methods used: Coaching, books, publications, media and workshops.

- Vision: Successful and prosperous entrepreneurs in Africa

You can contact Paul on the following email address:

Email: pketa@team6.co.za

18 Bibliography

[1]   New International Version, Holy Bible.

[2]   King James, Holy Bible.

[3]   CWR, "www.cwr.org.uk," [Online].

[4]   Institute for Motivational Living, "DISC Profile".

[5]   Dr. William Marston, "https://discprofile.com/what-is-disc/william-marston/," [Online].

[6]   D. W. Dyer, "http://brainyquote.com/quotes/authors/w/wayne_dyer_2.html," [Online].

[7]   R. W. E. Paul, "http://blog.gaiam.com/quotes/authors/ralph-waldo-emerson/65882," [Online].

[8]   The Institute for Motivational Living, The TEAMS Profile.

[9]   The Institute for Motivational Living, The Values Style Profile.

[10]   Norman Vincent Peale.

[11]   Doctor John Stanko, "Discover your purpose".

[12]   Paul Keta, "http://www.team6.co.za," Team Six Consultants. [Online].

[13]   The Institute for Motivational Living, The Biblical Personality System.

[14]   "http://www.wilywalnut.com/," [Online].

[15]   "http://brainyquote.com/quotes/quotes/t/thomashuxl400102.html," [Online].

www.ingramcontent.com/pod-product-compliance
Lightning Source LLC
Chambersburg PA
CBHW060740050426
42449CB00008B/1275

* 9 7 8 0 6 2 0 6 5 0 3 1 1 *